Notes for Serials Cataloging

Notes for Serials Cataloging

Compiled by

Nancy G. Thomas
Serials Cataloger, Ohio State University

and

Rosanna O'Neil
Head, Copy Cataloging Section,
Automated Processing Department
Ohio State University

Edited by
Arlene G. Taylor

1986
Libraries Unlimited, Inc. — Littleton, Colorado

LIBRARIES UNLIMITED, INC.
P.O. Box 263
Littleton, Colorado 80160-0263

Library of Congress Cataloging-in-Publication Data

Thomas, Nancy G.
  Notes for serials cataloging.

  Bibliography: p. 122
  1. Cataloging of serial publications. 2. Notes
(Cataloging)--Specimens. 3. Anglo-American cataloguing
rules. 4. Descriptive cataloging--Rules. I. O'Neil,
Rosanna, 1957-   . II. Taylor, Arlene G., 1941-   .
III. Title.
Z695.7.T46   1986   025.3'432   86-9
ISBN 0-87287-535-0

To Jeanne Magill
N.G.T.

To my mother, Giuliana Simeoni O'Neil
R.O.

Contents

Contents

Foreword

Nancy G. Thomas and Rosanna O'Neil have created a work that will assist serials catalogers in a way not provided in any other source. While other works provide examples of notes using various AACR2 rules, this work arranges the examples by MARC tag. In tagging manuals there are usually a few examples for each tag; here there are numerous examples arranged by function of note.

This work is also unique in providing relationships among similar kinds of notes. For example, under tag 525, section IV, for updates that are supplements, the reader is referred to tag 500 for updates that are not supplements and to tag 580 for named updates. This feature will be of immense assistance to students who, because they find the complex relationships and terminology of serials almost overwhelming, have difficulty determining which field of a MARC record to use in various situations. The feature will also, no doubt, assist practicing librarians in the same way. Finally, the work goes beyond any other source in providing examples of complex notes that deal with unusual situations. Most sources provide examples only of the more common types of notes applicable to many situations.

It is a pleasure to edit a work whose authors are as knowledge-able, thorough, and careful as Thomas and O'Neil. The work is a significant addition to a sizeable group of cataloging manuals.

Arlene G. Taylor

Preface

The idea of putting together a compilation of notes used in serials cataloging came to us over lunch one day in 1983. As experienced serials catalogers, we knew that constructing a note that clearly and concisely describes the situation in hand can be the most frustrating part of cataloging a serial. At that time the only available tool offering help for this problem had been published over thirty years before.* While still useful, it was hardly appropriate when using AACR2 cataloging rules. So, we set about putting together a ready-reference tool to give serials catalogers examples to help them compose notes to suit their needs.

We strove to be consistent in punctuation, etc., and to that end we consulted with Dorothy Glasby, Assistant Chief, Serials Records Division, Library of Congress, to whom we are very grateful for her helpful and willing responses. The Ohio State University Libraries' policy of allowing faculty research time, as well as the financial assistance from the Office of the Vice-President for Research and Graduate Studies, was a substantial factor in our attaining our goal. Our supervisors were understanding and supportive in allowing us to be away from our jobs in order to make use of our research time, and make use of it we did! To say the least, the research involved, as well as the organizing, typing, etc., was quite a task, but we feel it was more than worth it. What you have in your hands is a meticulously prepared reference tool filled with the more complex types of notes that we found in *New Serial Titles,* OCLC records, or in our own original cataloging. We hope it will help to guide the serials cataloger to that ever-elusive perfect expression of what "that crazy serial has done this time!"

*Ruth Schley and Jane B. Davies, *Serials Notes Compiled from Library of Congress Cards Issued 1947-April 1951* (New York: Columbia University Libraries, 1952).

Introduction

Notes for Serials Cataloging is a selective compilation of notes to be used as examples in constructing that ever-elusive "perfect note." These notes were chosen from the following sources: (1) *New Serial Titles,* August 1982-May 1984, (2) OCLC serial records, and (3) our own cataloging.

In compiling this list, we selected notes that could be discerned as generic; those which, with a little adaptation, could be applied to many serials. Though some of the notes are basic, most of what we have selected depict the more complex situations in the life of a serial.

Since the information provided in the notes area is, for the most part, considered free-language, we are not necessarily prescribing how a note should be constructed, but rather we are providing the creative cataloger with examples on which to base the creation of her/his own notes. For instance, "Text in Italian," "In Italian," and "Articles in Italian" are basically all saying the same thing and are all appropriate. The choice is subjective; there is no prescribed rule. Such rules do exist, however, in the punctuation of most notes, and it is in this area that we have striven to be consistent (see our comments on editing, below).

ORGANIZATION OF THE NOTES

Since so many libraries are currently cataloging serials using the MARC format, we have organized the various types of notes by MARC field based on the definitions of the fields as found in OCLC's *Serials Format,* 2nd ed., and LC's *MARC Serials Editing Guide* as revised and updated through June 1984. For the more complex fields, we have provided our own topical subdivisions in order to make it easier for the cataloger to find the appropriate example. Each chapter is preceded by a brief description of the scope of the field taken from the OCLC *Serials Format,* 2nd ed. Then follows an outline which details the topical subarrangement of the notes found in the field.

We realize that the applicability of a given note may depend on the peculiarity of the serial. Therefore, in certain cases explanatory notes have been added in square brackets below the entry. At times it may be desirable to read the note in the context of the record in which it appears. For this purpose we have included a list of Sources. This list includes the title, the Library of Congress card number (LCCN), and the OCLC record number for the cataloging record from which the note was taken. While the OCLC number would be of use solely to those who have access to OCLC terminals, those libraries using other online cataloging systems will find the LCCN of use. We hope that most notes will be self-explanatory.

MARC FIELDS COVERED (AND NOT COVERED)

In general we have omitted notes which consist of direct quotes from the serial itself or which are created by using standard phrases plus information taken from the serial. For example, notes which begin with "Description based on:," "Cover title:," "Spine title:," and other such phrases have not been included. Likewise basic notes that can be generated from the linking fields 780 (Preceding Entry) and 785 (Succeeding Entry) have also been excluded. However, notes containing more complex linking information can be found in the chapter entitled "580 (Linking Entry Complexity Note)."

Frequency notes have also been excluded since the frequency information for a serial record is taken directly from the piece itself when available. For example, if one title states "Two no. a year," another says "Two issues yearly," and yet another states "Two times a year," the corresponding record would reflect what the pieces prescribed. We, therefore, felt that the inclusion of the 310 (Current Frequency) and 321 (Former Frequency) fields was not necessary for this compilation of notes.

Based on our personal experience we decided that the following fields would be those areas where the serials cataloger would most appreciate a little assistance:

500 (General Note)
515 (Numbering Peculiarities Note)
525 (Supplement Note)
530 (Additional Physical Forms Available Note)
533 (Photoreproduction Note)
546 (Language Note)
550 (Issuing Bodies Note)
555 (Cumulative Index Note/Finding Aids)
580 (Linking Entry Complexity Note)

Please note the exclusion of the 520 (Summary, Abstract, Annotation, Scope and Contents Note) field. The definition in the *MARC Serials Editing Guide* (revised March/April 1982) is as follows:

> This field contains unformatted notes that give information describing the scope and contents of the work. This could be a summary, abstract, annotation or only a phrase describing the work. Such information appears after the word "Summary:" on the printed cards. This word is not included in the record.
>
> The field is limited to formal summary statements. Informal summary notes are recorded in field 500. Notes which cite a related publication are recorded in field 580. (N.B. Both of these kinds of notes were recorded in field 520 prior to AACR 2.)

Since the definition has been narrowed to such an extent, the field is seldom used. We found that many of the 520s we had selected to include in the compilation were tagged before the redefinition of this field and, therefore, no longer belonged there. These notes have been retagged and put into the appropriate fields.

There are certain kinds of notes that may belong in more than one field or fit into more than one topical subdivision due to the complexity of the note. We recommend becoming familiar with the arrangement of the book, and when searching for a note, considering this possibility. When possible, we have referred the user to the other subdivision(s) or field(s) that might be of interest.

EDITING OF THE NOTES

We stated earlier that, although the note area is basically a free-language area, some uniformity in punctuation is necessary and prescribed by *AACR2* and the other cataloging manuals. Many notes, though having current and useful information, had to be updated according to the present punctuation standards. With the inception of AACR2 some of the terminology has also changed. For instance, it was necessary in the 546 (Language Note) field to change the word "or" to the word "and" as appropriate to that serial title.

After very closely reviewing the OCLC *Serials Format,* 2nd ed., and the LC *MARC Serials Editing Guide*, we discovered that the tagging in the OCLC records of some notes was either outdated (as in the 520 field) or simply mistagged. In these instances we reassigned the notes to the appropriate field numbers.

Much of the editing that was done to the notes was done in order to be as consistent as possible in the construction and tagging of the notes, and to reflect the most current interpretation of the various note fields used in serials cataloging.

We hope you will find *Notes for Serials Cataloging* to be an integral part of your serials reference collection.

500

General Note

SCOPE

"Field 500 contains unformatted notes that give bibliographic information not present elsewhere in the record, or information that is present elsewhere but that must be repeated in field 500 to generate an intelligible note. Use field 500 for any note for which no specific tag has been defined." — OCLC *Serials Format,* 2nd ed.

ARRANGEMENT

I. Informal Summary/Scope Notes

    A. Summary statements
    B. General contents information
    C. "Includes" statements
    D. Proceedings information
    E. General coverage information
    F. General translation notes

II. Notes About Titles

    A. Title proper information
    B. Other title information
    C. Language of title/parallel title information
    D. Names of titles within a serial (not issued separately)
    E. Varying forms of title
    F. Alternate issues

III. Imprint Variation Information

IV. Issuing Information

    A. Format
    B. Updates and revisions
    C. Miscellaneous issuing information

V. Miscellaneous General Notes

500   GENERAL NOTE

I.   INFORMAL SUMMARY/SCOPE NOTES

A.   Summary statements
1.   A guide to current programs.
2.   A union list of art serials in research libraries in the Washington, D.C. metropolitan area.
3.   Abstracts of C.S.I.R.O. published papers, transactions.
4.   A series of monographs and studies on the history of cartography, reprinted from periodicals since 1800.
5.   List of acquisitions to the Society's library.
6.   Index of articles about Hong Kong in selected Hong Kong periodicals.
7.   Annual update for Arkansas five year state plan.
8.   Unacc. melodies; includes chord symbols.
9.   Combined biennial reports of agencies which administer Washington State's human resources programs and services.
10.   Each vol. gives biographical sketches of persons in various aspects of mass communications, each aspect appearing as a subtitle.
11.   No. 1-13 are short-term studies; with no. 14 becomes a series of supplementary reports summarizing the results of longer term data collection.

B.   General contents information
1.   Lists names, addresses and work in progress of all members.
2.   Third issue of each vol. contains a list of members.
3.   Looseleaf including: newsletter, evaluations, new releases and cumulative index.
4.   Each year consists of 1 list of documents and 1 index.
5.   Vols. for each year comprised of preliminary and main tables, 1974-   ; summary and main tables.
6.   Some issues devoted to individual authors.
7.   Each convocation devoted to one aspect of accounting.
8.   Each issue covers a different subject.
9.   Each issue covers a particular geographic area or city.
10.   Vols. 1-   have a regional focus, e.g., v. 1: The West.
11.   One issue each year consists of an annual conference review.
12.   The Oct. issue of each year is the annual report of the Association.

13. Fourth quarter issue contains also the annual report for the fiscal year.
14. Consists of reprints of journal articles.
15. Content of yearbooks originates in the sessions of the International Conference on Education (ICE). -

C. "Includes" statements*
   1. Includes syllabus paragraphs of the opinions of the Attorney General of Ohio as they are released.
   2. Includes printed introduction and bibliographic key.
   3. Includes reproduction of t.p. and plates; text in Japanese translation, with notes in Japanese added.
   4. Vols. 1-6 include music; v. 7-17 consist exclusively of actual music without articles on musical subjects.
   5. Some numbers include reports submitted to Its general meeting.
      [Title: Bulletin of the International Social Security Association]
   6. Vols. 9-17 include decisions of the War Labor Board.
   7. Vol. for 1980 includes index for 1977-1979 of ALEC's suggested state legislation.
   8. Issues for May 1894-May 1908 include index to annotations of the Lawyers' reports, annotated.
   9. One folded map included.
   10. Some issues include Appendixes; some Appendixes issued under separate cover.

D. Proceedings information
   1. Consists of proceedings of symposia.
   2. Consists of proceedings of meetings on biomaterials.
   3. Consists of proceedings of meetings held in various places.
   4. Proceedings of various symposia held 1978-
   5. Some proceedings cover both spring and fall meetings.
   6. Vols. 1-   based on the proceedings of a series of workshops.
   7. Vols. 1-   consist of papers presented at an American Chemical Society Symposium.
   8. Vols. 1-   include 6th-   proceedings of the annual conference.
   9. Vols. 1-   are the Proceedings of the Brown University Symposium on the Biology of Skin, 1959-
   10. Vols. 1-2 constitute proceedings of: Symposium on the Fracture Mechanics of Ceramics; 3-   proceedings of: International Symposium on the Fracture Mechanics of Ceramics.

---

*For similar examples which involve separately published titles, see "580 Linking Entry Complexity Note."

11. Consists of the proceedings of the 6th-   meeting of the International Society of Hypertension.
12. Consists of papers presented at a postgraduate course in advanced geriatric medicine in Glasgow, Nov. 1980-
13. Includes the papers and proceedings of the annual conference of the Australian Mining and Petroleum Law Association.
14. Includes programs and brief proceedings of 1st-32nd annual meetings, 1911-1946 (the Society was inactive 1918-1921). No meeting was held in 1944-1945.
15. Vols. for 1898-1941, 1948-1956 include the Society's proceedings (primarily abstracts of papers presented at the 10th-53rd annual meetings, and the 1948-1956 fall meetings).
16. Vols. for 1980-   include abstracts of proceedings of the 18th-   Annual Conference of the Australian Association of Clinical Biochemists.

E. General coverage information*
1. Data based on previous year.
2. Some issues include data from previous time periods.
3. Vols. for   include comparative data from previous years.
4. Vol. for 1980 is cumulative for 1978-1980.
5. Includes revised data for varying numbers of years.
6. Includes preliminary data and projections for the following two years.
7. Work objectives and proposals for 12-month period beginning July 1, and accomplishments for prior 12 months.
8. Issues for 1981/1982-   include bibliographies for reports published the preceding year.
9. Each issue covers films released the previous year as well as some films of the past.
10. Lists publications received and registered in the University Library in 1981 irrespective of date and place of publication, and includes also items published after 1975 not previously listed.
11. Each issue includes a bibliography of art books published in the United Kingdom during the preceding quarter; issue for Mar. 1982 covers books published June-Dec. 1981.

---

*For report year coverage information, see "515 Numbering Peculiarities Note."

12. Vol. for 1980 covers the results of the research conducted in the last 5 years beginning 1976.
13. Beginning with no. 650 each hundredth number contains a list of the reports and memoranda published since the last list.
14. Includes a five year plan for the following five years and an accountability report for the previous year.
15. Includes trends for the current year and the four preceding years.
16. Covers events of the previous seven years, e.g., vol. for 1981 covers 1974-1980, etc.
17. Each no. will index articles published during the semester preceding the issue of the Index.
18. Vol. for 1975 indexes publications of the U.S. Geological Survey, 1879-1974.
19. Issue for Mar. 1981 contains index for Jan.-Mar. 1981 in microfiche form.

F. General translation notes*
    1. Cover-to-cover translation from Russian.
    2. Articles translated from Russian periodicals.
    3. English translation of German work.
    4. English language translation of papers originally written in Russian.
    5. Translations of articles from Chinese publications.
    6. Translations of articles from major Chinese physics and astronomy journals.
    7. Translation of papers from Soviet and Eastern European periodicals.
    8. Chiefly English translations of articles originally in Portuguese selected from publications of the Instituto de Pesquisas.
    9. English abstracts of anthropological publications in German, and of publications by Austrian, and Swiss authors in languages other than German.
    10. Contains English abstracts of original papers and letters to the editor that appear in the Japanese edition.
    11. First issue each year devoted to translations into English; the second, into all other languages.

---

*For notes concerning language(s) of text, see "546 Language Note."

II. NOTES ABOUT TITLES

A. Title proper information
1. Title from letter of transmittal.
2. Title from table of contents page.
3. Title from the cover or spine.
4. Title from the case supplied by the publisher of reprint edition.
5. Title appears only on the colophon of many issues.
6. Each title includes the name of a municipality (e.g., Analisis geoeconomico Atoyac, Analisis geoeconomico Atotonilco El Alto, etc.).
    [Title: Analisis geoeconomico . . .]
7. Vols. for 1982-   carry in the title the year of issue, i.e. Compensation 82.
8. Each issue carries also in its title the number of articles, e.g., Seks faglige bidrag.
9. Vols. for   have title only in characters.
10. Some issues lack title.
11. Later reports issued without title.
12. Vol. for 1978 issued without title.
13. First issue was untitled when first published and was reprinted in Dec. 1969.
14. Vol. 56, no. 5 has an additional cover bearing its former title.

B. Other title information
1. Some issues lack the other title information.
2. Some numbers have subtitle: Midwest edition.
3. Subtitle varies; some numbers issued without subtitle.
4. Subtitle varies to reflect the titles incorporated.
5. Subtitle fluctuates between Ergänzungsband and Supplement depending upon the language of the issue.
6. Vol. for 1981/82 has subtitle: Demand, productivity, and population.
7. Each issue has a distinctive title.
8. Each vol. has also a distinctive title that varies from year to year.
9. Each issue also has a theme title.
10. Vol. 1 also carries distinctive title: Urth' ap-1.
11. Issues for vols. 86-87 of 1977-1978 also bear individual titles (Chemical sciences, Earth and planetary sciences, etc.) indicating contents of the issue.

C. Language of title/parallel title information*
   1. Title also appears in other languages.
   2. Order of titles varies.
   3. Title order varies frequently.
   4. Order of titles alternates.
   5. Order of series titles varies.
   6. Order of titles on title page rotates each year.
   7. Order of titles varies with language of text.
   8. Titles also in Eurostat's other official languages.
   9. Finnish title precedes the Latin one in v. 1-25.
  10. Reports for 1974-1975, 1976-1977, and 1977-1978 have title in English preceding title in Afrikaans.
  11. Vols. for Jan./June 1953-v. 5, no. 15 have parallel title: Philatelist.
  12. Some bilingual English and French numbers issued with parallel title: Rapport technique/Programme "bonite."
  13. Parallel title varies: Income and product, Puerto Rico, 1981-
  14. Parallel title dropped with issue for Jan. 1971.
  15. No. 6-   dropped parallel titles.
  16. English title only, 1964-1968; 1980-
  17. Translated title: Selected gems in medicine.

D. Names of titles within a serial (not issued separately)†
   1. Includes section entitled: Tax laws enacted.
   2. Some issues include an unpaged section: Transport research bulletin.
   3. Every third year, 1980-   includes section: Prevention profile.
   4. Each issue includes separate but continuously paged sections called: Nuclear medicine; and: Ultrasound.
   5. Includes section "Geographischer Literaturbericht" (title varies) which was issued as a separately paged suppl. to v. 32-55, 1886-1909.
   6. Vols. for 197 -   include Edunet news, a separately paged section with its own numbering.
   7. Contains two sections: Coin news, and: Medal news, which have separate caption titles and pagings, 1981-
   8. Issues for   include insert: Index to selected stars.
   9. Includes booklet: Preface and list of contributing libraries ([8 p.] ; 11 x 15 cm.).

*For notes concerning language(s) of text, see "546 Language Note."

†For names of titles within a serial issued separately, see "580 Linking Entry Complexity Note."

10. Issue for Apr. 1976 includes: John W. Dawes family directory.
11. One issue each year consists of a buyers' guide called "Green Book."
12. Each vol. comprised of one issue each of: Colt American handgunning and Gutmann knife journal, and two issues of: Scubapro diving & snorkeling.
    [Title: Aqua-field sportsman]
13. Vols. for   consist of: Alphabetical directory, Geographical directory, Areas of interest code, with those for 1979-1980 containing also: By-laws.

E. Varying forms of title
   1. Title varies slightly.
   2. Other slight variations in title.
   3. Title alternates irregularly: Relatório.
      [Title: Relatório anual]
   4. In the editorial for v. 1, no. 1 called: Journal of oil and petroleum pollution.
   5. July issue called Distribution guide issue.
   6. Winter number also has title: Studies by members of SCMLA.
   7. Vol. 6 has title: Current trends in life science.
      [Title: Current trends in life sciences]
   8. Some no. have title: Racial ethnic brotherhood.
   9. Some issues are cumulations with title: Anuario bibliográfico ecuatoriano.
   10. One issue each volume, v. 6-   called also: Ninth Circuit survey; one issue each volume, v. 8-   called also: Women's law forum.
   11. Beginning in 1980 some issues have title: Knitting times newsweekly.   One issue each month, Mar. 24, 1980-   has title: Apparel world.
   12. Sometimes published as: Mississippi game & fish.
       [Title: Mississippi game and fish]
   13. Vols. for even-numbered years have title: National accounts.
   14. Variant title appearing only on title-page of 37: Acta mathematica naturalium Universitatis Comenianae.
   15. Title in colophon of dai 2-gŏ, published in 1982 in romanization: Haiku Bungakkan kiyo.
   16. Vol. 22, no. 2 called Legislative research checklist due to printing error.
       [Title: State government research checklist]

F. Alternate issues*
1. Alternating issues called ORSA/TIMS bulletin.
[Title: TIMS/ORSA bulletin]
2. Alternate issues have title: South African journal for librarianship and information science.
3. Alternate issues titled: Geology and geography; Geophysics and geodesy.
4. Alternate years have title: Revision of occupational trends in the State of Oregon.
5. Composed of alternately issued vols. with subtitles: Fundamentals; Applications; Equipment; and: Systems.
6. Vols. for 1973-   include: International monographs on early child care, as alternate issues of the journal.
7. Beginning in 19- -   monthly issues issued alternately as Brewers edition and Wholesaler edition; weekly issues issued as tabloid with edition statement varying.

III. IMPRINT VARIATION INFORMATION†

1. Distributor information taken from label.
2. Imprint varies: Vol. 3-   published in Beaumont, Tex.
3. Imprint varies: New York : Columbia University Press, c1933-
4. Place of publication varies.
5. Publisher and place of publication vary with each edition.
[Imprint: S.l. : s.n.]
6. Published: Budapest : Lehrbuchverlag, 1979-
[Imprint: Budapest : Magyar Néprajzi Társaság, 1975-   ]
7. No. 1-5 published in New York; New ser., v. 1, no. 1-v. 4, no. 2 published in Boston, Mass.
[Imprint: New York : . . .]
8. Vols. for 1975/76-   published: London : Studio Vista ; New York : Van Nostrand Reinhold.
9. Issued at: Salem State College, Salem, MA, Oct. 1981-
[Imprint: New York, N.Y. : CORD, 1981-   ]

---

*For notes concerning numbering shared with other titles, see "515 Numbering Peculiarities Note."

†For publication information in regard to issuing bodies, see "550 Issuing Bodies Note."

IV. ISSUING INFORMATION

A. Format
 1. Reproduced from typed catalog cards.
 2. Some no. reproduced from typescript; some no. loose-leaf.
 3. In loose-leaf folders.
 4. Loose-leaf for monthly updating.
 5. Loose-leaf for updating between editions.
 6. Beginning with v. 2, current issues in loose-leaf format; each vol. issued also in bound form after completion.
 7. Issued as advance sheets replaced periodically by bound vols.
 8. First number of each month issued in magazine format; all other numbers have variant title: NAHB builder newspaper.
 9. Published in journal-sized folders containing microfiches (10.5 x 15 cm.).
 10. Vols. for Sept. 1980   issued in newspaper format.
 11. Vols. published in 1975-   shelved in binder with spine title: Discussion memoranda.
 12. Vols. for 1978-   issued also in softcover edition with the cover title: Access: law.
 13. Introduction is not available in microform; it is available only in printed form.

B. Updates and revisions*
 1. Half-yearly updates.
 2. Kept up-to-date with loose-leaf revisions.
 3. Kept up-to-date with annual replacement pages.
 4. Updated by replacement pages and cumulated irregularly.
 5. Update issued between editions.
 6. Kept up-to-date between editions with revision pages.
 7. Each edition is kept up-to-date by quarterly cumulated releases.
 8. Updates the base volume published in 1971.
 9. Updated monthly, may be updated by German/French/ Dutch edition also.
 10. Vols. 1-2 are updated annually; v. 3 will be revised only as necessary.
 11. Five year updates are planned.
 12. Each issue updates preceding issue.
 13. Each list is an addendum to the previous list.

---

*For updates that are supplements, see "525 Supplement Note"; for named updates, see "580 Linking Entry Complexity Note."

14. Vol. 1, Federal laws, replaces the opinions published in the loose-leaf binder v. 5, Decisions, from v. 1, 1970-
15. First issue of each vol. constitutes main annual publication; issues no. 2-4 are updates.

C. Miscellaneous issuing information
   1. Limited edition of 350 copies.
   2. Issued each year in preliminary and in final form.
   3. Vols. 1-4 issued only on an experimental basis (not for sale).
   4. Abstracts also issued biweekly in computer printout form, Jan. 1983-
   5. The preface in no. 4 (1979) indicates that no. 1-3 were published under an earlier title.
   6. No. 1 is a reprint of the original issue which was privately printed; it contains the archaeological papers only, the preliminary matter (p. 1-54) being omitted.
   7. Some issues consist, wholly or in part, of preprints.
   8. Issued one year after publication of the Russian original.
   9. Issued also in an annual summary.
   10. Annual summary included with the 1st quarterly report.
   11. Includes separate classified section, published fortnightly.
   12. Each vol. published in separate fasc., each devoted to a particular subject, i.e., Zheleznitsi.
   13. Beginning with fall 1982, for sale by the Supt. of Docs.
   14. Some issues not for sale by Supt. of Docs.
   15. Information incorrect in document as to for sale by the Supt. of Docs.
   16. Many subseries issued within this publication.
   17. Size varies: Vol. 1, no. 2-   : 36 cm.

V. MISCELLANEOUS GENERAL NOTES

1. Description based on surrogate.
2. Description based on surrogate of: No. 1.
3. Ceased with Dec. 1980 issue. Cf. Letter from publisher.
4. At head of title: Centre national de la recherche scientifique, Centre régional de publications de Meudon-Bellevue, 1979-
5. Individual issues of copy from which fiche was made lack title pages.
6. Contents alternate monthly: Original articles in odd-numbered months; Current literature in even-numbered months.
7. "Confidential," 1970-1975.
8. Desk copy.
9. Chiefly tables.
10. Part of the illustrative matter is folded.

11. Part of the illustrative material in pocket.
12. Map on folded leaf in pocket.
13. Some issues have different cochairmen.
14. Errata slip inserted in 1981 edition.
15. Vols. for 1980-   are printed for the use of the Committees on Foreign Affairs and on Science and Technology; 1981 was printed for the use of the Committee on Foreign Affairs.
16. Vols. for 19   have section and separate t.p. in Arabic.
17. A project supported by grants in aid from the National Geographic Society.
18. Each edition has Ernst & Whinney stock number.
19. Issues prior to Jan. 1978 were classed: A 89.8:(v.nos.&nos.); issues for Jan. 1978-Sept. 1980 were classed: A 105.19:(v.nos.nos.).
20. Issued with United Nations publications sales no.
21. Yearbooks for 1948-   issued with the United Nations publications sales no.: 1949.XIII.1.
22. Prior to Jan. 1976 issues were classed C56.216:MQ-22 during the time the Census Bureau was subordinate to the Social and Economic Statistics Administration.
23. Intended audience: Junior and senior high school librarians.
24. For the professional interior designer, architect, and contract specifier in the 17 western states.
25. Sometimes referred to as: Blue-covered section.
26. Not to be confused with an earlier publication of the same name, issued in Santiago de Chile.
27. Not to be confused with an earlier title of the same name published 1976 by F.A. Davis.
28. This series of Proceedings is independent of the earlier one of the same title, published in 3 parts, 1877-1895.
29. Published as: Bicentennial edition, 1975.
30. Earlier vols. also issued as departmental ed.

515
Numbering
Peculiarities Note

SCOPE

"Field 515 contains unformatted notes citing report year coverage or irregularities and peculiarities in numbering." — OCLC *Serials Format,* 2nd ed.

ARRANGEMENT

   I. Report Year Coverage

  II. Double Numbering

 III. Combined Issues or Volumes

 IV. Numbering Inconsistencies or Irregularities
- A. Numbering lacking
- B. Numbering dropped
- C. Numbering added
- D. Numbering errors
- E. Numbering shared with other titles
- F. Numbering that does not begin with vol. 1
- G. Inconsistencies in chronological designations
- H. Miscellaneous numbering inconsistencies or irregularities

  V. Issuing Peculiarities
- A. General issuing peculiarities
- B. Number of issues per volume, etc.
- C. Issued in named parts, sections, etc.
- D. Issued in unnamed parts, sections, etc.
- E. Multiple or revised editions
- F. Cumulations

 VI. Preliminary Issues

VII. Suspension of Publication

VIII. Items not Published

515   NUMBERING PECULIARITIES NOTE

I.   REPORT YEAR COVERAGE*

1. Each report covers 5 years.
2. Report covers fourth quarter data.
3. Report year ends Mar. 31 of the following year.
4. Period covered by reports is current and previous school year.
5. Periods covered by reports correspond to the academic years.
6. Each report covers four quarters for the year: Oct.-Sept.
7. Vols. for 1977-   cover calendar year and first half of following year.
8. Reports for Apr. 1979/Mar. 1980-   cover Japanese fiscal years 1979-
9. Report covers financial year ending Dec. 31 of the preceding year.
10. Report covers first half of fiscal year; the Treasurer's annual report covers second half of fiscal year.
11. Each report covers 2 years and is published at the end of marketing season for the various states.
12. Report year irregular; first report covers Jan. 1938-Sept. 1939.
13. Report years for equalized assessed valuations and tax rates vary.
14. Each report contains cumulated monthly summaries covering an eight year period, i.e., 1967-1975.
15. Report for   includes projected statistics for
16. Report cumulative for four quarters of the State fiscal year,   ; for the first two quarters of State fiscal year,
17. First report year covers period Apr. 5, 1978-Dec. 31, 1978.
18. Vol. for 1979 covers Apr. 1 through Dec. 31.   Succeeding issues cover calendar year.
    [Title: Annual report]
19. Report for 1979 covers 3 years, i.e., 1979-1981.
20. Report for 1979 includes summary data for 1975-1978.

---

*For general coverage information, see "500 General Note."

21. First report covers a three-year period; subsequent annual reports cover five-year periods.
22. Period covered by report for 1970/72 ends July 30; report year for 1972/73-   ends Apr. 30.

II. DOUBLE NUMBERING

1. Vols. also bear numbering in Dutch.
2. Two systems of numeric designation start with issue 7.
3. Issues carry also whole numbering.
4. Also numbered within each presidency.
5. No. 1-2 called 1. année; no. 1 called also v. 1, fasc. 1.
6. Issues for 1980/81-1981/82 called also Part II.
7. Vols. for Mar./June 1965-   called also New series.
8. Nr. 13-   called also anul 11-
9. Vols. for winter 1979-   called also issue #5-
10. Vols. for 1982-   called also anno 1-   = ser. 1-
11. Vols. for 1978- called also 6th annual report-
12. Vols. for 1980-   called also v. 15-   in continuation of the numbering of: Ocologia plantarum.
13. Vol. 1, no. 1-   called also v. 13, no. 1-   continuing the numbering designation of the previous title.
14. Vol. 1 (1983)-   called also: Chemical geology, v. 41 (1983)-   in continuation of parent journal.
15. No. 1-3 called also v. 3, no. 1-2 and v. 4, no. 3 in continuation of ser. IV of the council's studies which this succeeds.
16. Also numbered [50]-   in the main series: Commentationes physico-mathematicae.
17. Issues carry also whole no. in parentheses, continuing numbering of "Gazeta Vremennogo rabochego i krestĩanskogo pravitel'stva."
18. Has also whole numbers (odd numbers 589-   assigned to Faraday transactions 1; even numbers assigned to Faraday transactions 2).
19. Issued irregularly in parts which, in v. 1-54 are numbered consecutively no. 1-220; in later vols. the consecutive numbering was discontinued.
20. Each issue carries also numbering derived from the initials of its author, e.g., NNM-1-'82.
21. Reports also numbered serially within list of all the Commission's reports.
22. Some no. are also numbered as suppl. to the parent journal: Allergy.
23. Some issues carry also the date of the Jewish calendar.
24. Both Christian and Hegira dates appear on pieces, but vol. designation follows Hegira dates.

III. COMBINED ISSUES OR VOLUMES

1. Some issues combined.
2. Some numbers issued together.
3. Some numbers issued in combined form.
4. Some issues published in combined form.
5. Two sections issued together once a month.
6. Vol. 5, no. 1-4 issued combined.
7. Report for 1974/76 published in combined form in 1976.
8. Vols. for spring & summer 1979 and spring & summer 1982, issued in combined form.
9. Vol. 1, no. 1-4 (summer 1982-spring 1983) published together in one volume.
10. Issued in combined volumes for 1937-1942 and for 1942-1944; issued annually thereafter.
11. Vol. 4, no. 1 has stamp which reads: "The special double issue contains vol. 4, no. 1 & 2."
12. Each issue bears a combined numbering, e.g., no. 1-2.
13. Some reports published combined in one vol.; cover has dates of both years on it, although each report year has a separate part with its own title page.
14. Some no. published as combined issues with: Ethnic racial review.

IV. NUMBERING INCONSISTENCIES OR IRREGULARITIES

A. Numbering lacking
1. Some issues lack numbering.
2. First issue lacks numeric designation.
3. Later issues lack numbering.
4. Issue for May 1981 has no vol. numbering.
5. Vol. 1, no. 1-4 lack vol. and no. designations.
6. Issue for Oct. 1974 lacks numbering, but constitutes no. 169.
7. First issue is not numbered or dated but constitutes v. 1, no. 2.
8. Issues for Sept. 1979-   unnumbered but constitute ano 1, no. 1-
9. Issues for Nov. 1978-   carry no vol. number.
10. Issues for Sept. 1980-   lack vol. numbering but constitute v. 1, no. 1-
11. Vol. for 1980 lacks numeric and chronological designation.
12. First issue lacks numeric designation for the section title.
13. No. 1-4 lack title and numbering.
14. Earlier vols. are unnumbered and lack series title.
15. Some vols. lack series numbering.

16. Vols. 6-7 issued without series numbering; no. 183a, 183b assigned arbitrarily.
17. Some issues have no vol. numbering but are called "Special issue."
18. Special issues may be unnumbered.
19. The first three vols. identified by date only; the last two by no. only.
20. Issues have no vol. or no. designations.   Two issues may also carry the same month and year and not be duplicates.

B. Numbering dropped
1. Vol. numbering ceased with v. 21, 1975.
2. Numbering ceased with 3rd report, 1978-1979.
3. Beginning with no. 16 vol. numbering is dropped.
4. New series designation dropped with v. 7, 1980.
5. Issue numbering dropped with v. 5, fall 1981; vol. numbering dropped with winter 1982.
6. Vol. numbering ends with summer/fall 1978 issue; whole numbering begins with May 1979 issue.
7. Issues identified by vol. and no. and date through v. 4, no. 9/10, 1981; by vol. and date, v. 5, fall 1981; by date, winter 1982-
8. The monthly issues were numbered consecutively (without vol. no.) from the beginning of the series to no. 155, Feb. 1931; with the no. for Mar. 1931, the consecutive numbering was discontinued and a numbering by vols. was adopted, the vol. for 1931 being v. 16 as reckoned from the first year of issue.

C. Numbering added
1. Vol. numbering begins with Aug. 1978 issue.
2. Numbering began with v. 10, no. 4, May 1979.
3. Numbering includes vol. designation with first issue for 1978.
4. Issues 1 and 2 called Serial 1 and 2.   Vol. designation assumed with v. 3, June 1975.
5. Vol. numbering resumed with v. 20, no. 1, Jan. 1980.
6. Resumes the volume numbering of: Review of books and religion (Belmont, Vt.).
   [Numeric and chronological designation: Vol. 10, no. 1 (mid-Sept. 1981)-   ]
7. Issue numbers supplied beginning with v. 45.

D. Numbering errors
  1. 37th omitted in numbering.
  2. Vol. numbering irregular: v. 34 omitted; v. 41, no. 2-3 called v. 42, no. 2-3.
  3. Vol. 7, no. 7 repeated in vol. numbering.
  4. Vol. numbering irregular: occasional numbers repeated.
  5. Vol. numbering irregular: v. 28 repeated.
  6. Numbering for v. 1, no. 1 is repeated on issues for summer 1972 and for 1974.
  7. Weekly issue, Oct. 20, 1958 and monthly issue, Nov. 1958 both called v. 58, no. 11.
  8. Issues for Apr. 1970 and Sept. 1970 are both designated as instructional aid no. 45.
  9. Two reports numbered 45th: one covering the period from July 1-Dec. 31, 1925; the other for the calendar year 1926. Subsequent reports continue this numbering.
  10. Many issues misnumbered.
  11. Numbering very irregular.
  12. Frequent irregularities in numbering.
  13. Some irregularities in numbering; some numbers in v. 29 incorrectly numbered v. 30.
  14. Issue for 1978-79 incorrectly called 1977-78 on t.p.
  15. Issue for 1967 called 10-11, but constitutes 10 only.
  16. Vol. for 1979 constitutes 17th, but incorrectly marked 16th.
  17. Final issue called 1980 but constitutes final 1979 issue.
  18. Aug. 1977-   issues called v. 100, no. 1-   but constitute v. 99, no. 15- ; issues for Jan. 1978 repeat v. 100, no. 1-   corresponding to the numbering of NARD journal.
  19. Errors in numbering: v. 31, no. 2-3, Feb.-Mar. 1981 called v. 30, no. 2-3; v. 31, no. 5, May 1981 called v. 31, no. 4.
  20. Vol. 51, no. 610 incorrectly numbered v. 52, no. 610; correct numbering resumes with v. 51, no. 611.
  21. Vol. 2, no. 12 misnumbered as v. 2, no. 11; v. 2, no. 20-24 misnumbered as v. 2, no. 21-25.
  22. Issue for Dec. 14, 1981 erroneously numbered v. 4, no. 37, following the numbering sequence of: NAHB builder.
  23. Reprint edition covering Aug. 1938-Sept. 1939 numbered 1-299; erroneously printed as no. 1-229; no. 1 corresponds to no. 395 in the original numbering.
  24. Numbering irregular: issue for spring/summer 1978 called also no. 3; issue for winter 1982 called also v. 5, no. 2.
  25. The 44th regular session of the General Assembly was designated as the 45th regular session. The error in numbering has been continued by all the following assemblies.

26. Conferences for 1914-1916, previously not included in the numbering, published in 1974, thus calling the 51st the 54th conference.

E. Numbering shared with other titles*
   1. Vols. for 1958-1964, internumbered with: Issues.
   2. Issue numbering alternates with other Mitchell Manuals publications.
   3. Alternates vol. numbering with the Transactions of the Society of Mining Engineers of AIME and the Transactions of the Metallurgical Society of AIME.
   4. Published concurrently with Biomedicine; the even numbered vols. constitute Biomedicine, the odd numbered vols. constitute Biomedicine express.
   5. Numbering integrated with that of Ferroelectrics, Apr. 1982-   . New series has separate numbering: v. 1, no. 1, Aug. 1983.
   6. Vol. 21 (1983) shares numbering with: American studies international newsletter.
   7. Issues are internumbered among these sections: supplement no. 210-249 Section A, Pathology or Section B, Microbiology and immunology; no. 250-   Section A, Pathology; Section B, Microbiology; or Section C, Immunology.
   8. Beginning with   alternating issues are also designated A or B, i.e., Nov. 1978 issue called v. 52A, no. 6.
   9. Vol. numbering is part of a sequence which includes: Mutation research; Mutation research. Section on environmental mutagenisis and related subjects; Mutation research. Reviews in genetic toxicology; and: Mutation research. Genetic toxicology testing.

F. Numbering that does not begin with vol. 1
   1. First issue is no. 2, 1980.
   2. Vol. 4 begins with no. 10 to conform to new publishers' publishing year.
   3. The vol. numbering is that of the original journal.
   4. Adopts its vol. numbering from other editions of: Today's education.
   5. Numbering and dates of issues pertain to: Le Praticien. [Title: Le Praticien. Supplément au no . . .]

---

*For general notes concerning alternate issues, see "500 General Note."

6. Vols. called ser. 6 to continue the series numbering of the debates of Parliament; issued 1803-1981 as ser. 1-5.
7. Vols. for 1961-   called "nouvelle série" in continuation of: Notulae systematicae, ISSN 0374-9223.
8. Vol. 1, no. 1-4 called v. 104, no. 1-4 in continuation of the numbering of the Journal of experimental psychology.
9. Assumes the vol. numbering of: Annuaire international de l'éducation et de l'enseignement.
10. Assumes the vol. numbering of the parent periodical: Journal de physique.
11. Continues the numbering of Central-Zeitung für Optik und Mechanik.
    [Merger of: Central-Zeitung für Optik und Mechanik (Berlin, Germany); and, Deutsche optische Wochenschrift (1948)]
12. Assumes the series and vol. numbering of: Bollettino della Unione matematica italiana. Sezione A, and Sezione B.
13. Issue for Mar. 1953, constituting v. 1, no. 1, is numbered consecutively with American Association of Rehabilitation Therapists bulletin, as v. 3, no. 3.
14. Articles in issues for Jan. 1977-   numbered consecutively boletín no. 228-
15. Each article is individually numbered following the numbering designation begun with Estudios CIEPLAN.

G. Inconsistencies in chronological designations
    1. Issues lack dates.
    2. Some issues lack dates.
    3. Vols. for   lack year designation.
    4. Issues for 1966 lack chronological designations; issues for 1967 misnumbered v. 1.
    5. Vol. 2, issue 4-v. 3 without date.
    6. Vol. 1, no. 1 without date but issued Mar. [?] 1978.
    7. Issues for Feb. 1980-   omit name of month.
    8. Issues for Mar. 1971 and Aug. 1971 have only monthly designation.
    9. Cover and title page show different years.
    10. No. 1 has cover date: automne 1978.
        [Chronological designation: No 1 [Oct. 1978]-   ]
    11. Title page of 1975 vol. erroneously designated 1976.
    12. No. 56/58 published in 1980 but constitutes last three issues for 1978.
    13. Chronological designation from spine.

H. Miscellaneous numbering inconsistencies or irregularities
   1. Numbering of some vols. incomplete due to irregular publi-
       cation and combined issues.
   2. Vols. for winter 1983-   have number on spine only.
   3. Consists of even numbered issues only.
   4. Numbering begins each year with 1.
   5. Numbering is repeated each year.
   6. Issues also numbered within the year.
   7. Numbered 1-12 within each year, 1958-1963; numbered
       1-13, 1964-
   8. Vols. for 1963-1965 numbered consecutively.   Vols. for
       1966-1978 start with no. 1 with each new year.
   9. Issue numbering begins again following the publication of
       each ed. of: The Directory of directories.
   10. Publication started new designation system in 1946.
   11. With 1979 called 2nd ser.
   12. Publication of a 2nd ser. began in 1971; 3rd ser. began in
       1975.
   13. The "new series" appearing on the cover of each number is
       in reference to earlier publications of the Association.
   14. Vol. for Jan. 1976-Jan. 1978 called new ser., no. 1-22.   With
       issue for Feb. 1978 cumulative numbering resumes
       with no. 221.
   15. Vol. numbering changed in 1979 to coincide with New
       Guard.
       [Title: New guard bulletin]
   16. Vol. numbering sequenced with the numbering of the
       Russian original.
   17. Number of each issue includes initials of agency or other
       body for which the note was prepared.
   18. Numbering includes the letter A, Jan. 1978-Dec. 1980,
       i.e., v. 83, no. A12.
   19. Designated as pt. 1 whenever a corresponding supplement
       (called pt. 2) is issued.
   20. Monthly issues for 1906 called v. 1; annual cumulation for
       1906 called v. 2.
   21. Pilot weekly edition issued Sept. 15, 1958 as v. 1, no. 1.
       Beginning with Oct. 20, 1958-   issued as v. 58, no.
       11-   assuming numbering scheme of monthly
       issues. In Aug. 1966, weekly numbers issued as v. 17,
       no. 6-   while monthly issues continue former
       numbering scheme.   Monthly issues adopt numbering
       scheme of weekly issues, beginning with v. 21, no. 16
       (Apr. 20, 1970)-
   22. Mid-Sept. to mid-Oct. 1982 and mid-Oct. to mid-Nov. 1982,
       called opus 1, no. 1 and opus 1, no. 2 respectively.

23. Most vols. have no whole numbering; some vols. are numbered as parts of the whole series and/or as parts of the series of Eastern or Western conferences (e.g., Feb. 1956 called 9th Joint Conference and 4th Western Conference).

24. Issue no. for Dec. 1974-Dec. 1976 are continuous, i.e., v. 2 begins with no. 5.

V. ISSUING PECULIARITIES

A. General issuing peculiarities
1. Not issued in numerical order.
2. Vol. 17 comes between vols. 14 and 15.
3. Numbers not issued in chronological order.
4. Some numbers published out of chronological sequence.
5. Issued irregularly between the regular biennial sessions.
6. Vols. published consecutively, one each month, Oct. 1981-May 1982; autumn/winter 1982-   issued concurrently.
7. Extra issues called Gaceta extraordinaria del gobierno de Guatemala are published in continuous numbering sequence with regular issues.
8. Last issue of each vol. is an annual index.
9. Beginning in 1948 the last issue published in December of each year (except for 1958-1962 when it was the first issue in January) is called "Annual number."
10. Jan. 1981-Jan. 1982 publisher experimented with publishing multiple issues some months targeted for specific professional interests, with the result that there were 3 issues, Physician, Nursing, Industrial hygiene, each month from Jan.-Apr. 1981, 2 issues, Safety and Health, for Sept. 1981 and Jan. 1982.   The publisher has discontinued this practice.
11. Each annual issued supersedes all previous issues.
12. Vol. 1-   is reprint of no. 1-20-
13. No. 4 and 5 not included in reprint ed.
14. No. 1 (1978) is in a limited edition of 1000.
15. Issue for Dec. 1978-Jan. 1979 was originally issued as a letter without serial title or numbering; copies were later titled and numbered retrospectively as no. 1.
16. Issues for v. 87, though numbered sequentially, are paginated according to subject: Chemical sciences, Earth and planetary sciences, and Mathematical sciences.
17. Vols. for July 30, 1979-   sections are continuously paged but not all sections are issued with the same frequency, e.g., B8 is followed by A8.

18. No. 1 not published in English.
    [Title in English]
19. Vol. 2 published in 1979.
    [Imprint: . . ., 1980-   ]
20. Vol. 8, no. 33 issued 27th July 1979.
    [Numeric and chronological designation: Vol. 8,
    no. 31 (10th Aug. 1979)-   ]
21. Membership directory published every sixth year in lieu of
    the annual research volume.
22. Vols. for 1969-   called regular session;   called
    fiscal year.
23. First report called Quarterly report (July-Sept. 1980);
    2nd report called Six-month report (July-Dec. 1980); 3rd
    report called Third quarterly report (1980-81).
24. Called [Part] C, 1973-1979; the first three issues each year
    called [Part] C, and the last three called [Part] D,
    1980-
25. Issues are alternately called "Section A," "Section B," or
    "Section C."
26. Beginning with v. 11, 1978 issues alternately called Part A:
    Chemical analysis and Part B: Clinical and
    biochemical analysis.
27. Issues for Sept. 1965-Aug. 1967 called alternately: Series A,
    Sciences; Series B, Managerial, or Series C, Bulletin;
    for Sept. 1967-Aug. 1975 called, alternately: Theory or
    Application series.
28. In vols. for 1973-   odd numbered vols. cover Molecular
    aspects, even numbered vols. cover Cellular aspects.
    These vols. are published concurrently with one no.
    of each vol. issued each month, e.g., v. 131, no. 1 (Jan.
    1973) covers Molecular aspects, and v. 132, no. 1
    (Jan. 1973) covers Cellular aspects.
29. Published in two series: Scientific and Humanistic, which
    had alternating numbering.
30. Published also with variant vol. numbering and content "for
    official use only."
31. Articles in each vol. also published as separate no.
32. Vols. 1 and 2, indexing items published in 1980 and 1981,
    compiled retrospectively and issued as single cumu-
    lative issue for each year; beginning with v. 3,
    to be issued quarterly with the fourth issue being
    cumulative.

B. Number of issues per volume, etc.
   1. No. of issues per vol. varies.
   2. Six issues per vol.; numbering within vols. begins Jan.
      and July.

3. Each vol. consists of 4 numbers; number of vols. per year varies.
4. Each vol. contains three unnumbered issues.
5. Four issues constitute a vol.
6. Vol. 1 complete in one issue.
7. Statistics for 1977-1979 issued as one vol.
8. Only three issues published for 1979.
[Frequency: Monthly]
9. Only one vol. issued to cover years 1968-1972.
10. Vol. 1, no. 1 was the only issue published for 1976.

C. Issued in named parts, sections, etc.
1. Vol. for 1967 issued in 2 sections: Print and Television.
2. Issued in 2 parts: v. 1, Authors and titles; v. 2-3, Subjects.
3. The survey is published in two parts: the National Edition, in July, and the International Edition, in January.
4. Issued in 2 vols., the 2nd called Appendixes.
5. Vol. for 1980 published in two issues, one called 1980 midyear.
6. Issued in 2 vols., each with distinctive title: Vol. 1, Pre-colonial through reconstruction; Vol. 2, Reconstruction through the present.
7. Issues for 1969/74 published in 4 vols.; 1970/75-   in 9 vols. covering various geographical regions.
8. Vols. for 1952-1981-   issued in two vols.: v. 1, Main aggregates; v. 2, Detailed tables.   Vol. 2 does not cover same time period as v. 1 (e.g., v. 2 published in 1983 covers 1964-1981).
9. Each vol. issued in two sections of varying frequency: Section A, Short reviews, research papers and comments; and Section B, In-depth reviews.
10. Vols. for 1979-   issued in multi-volume parts: M-1-   : Media series; P-1-   : Product series.
11. Beginning with v. 26, 1964, divided into 2 parts: Social sciences and Humanities.   Each part will be published in alternate years as a separate vol.
12. Beginning with the 4th ed., a 3rd vol. (called New associa-tions and projects (varies)) is issued periodically in parts as an inter-edition supplement.

D. Issued in unnamed parts, sections, etc.
1. Issued in two vols. per year, 1981-
2. Issued in 2 vols., 2nd ed.-
3. Each edition consists of two individually released parts.
4. First edition has three parts issued at six-month intervals.

5. Fourth ed. issued in 4 vols. each devoted to a specific academic area.
6. Each vol. issued in 16 parts with also a distinctive title.
7. 1981 annual issue published in 3 vols.
8. Issues for 1981-   published in 2 vols.
9. Issue for May 1957 issued in 2 pts.; pt. 2 bears former title.
10. 1979-1981 issued in 2 pts., with pt. 2 on microfiche.
11. Two pts. to a vol., each pt. with special t.p. and, in v. 1-2, 99, 105, 114 with separate paging.
12. Beginning 1974 each edition published in more than one vol.
13. Each supplement issued in several vols.
14. Some issues appear in more than 1 fascicle.
15. Some issues issued in 2 or more vols.
16. Each cumulation published in 4 or more vols.
17. Issues for   published in 2 or more unnumbered vols.
18. Proceedings for   issued in 2 or more vols.
19. Vols. for   issued in pts., each covering a different topic.
20. Vols. for 1968-   published in several issues, each issue covering one county.
21. Issued in pts. continuously paged and supplied with a general t.p. and subject index to form a vol.

E. Multiple or revised editions
1. Each vol. issued in multiple editions.
2. Revision issued annually.
3. Includes a 2nd ed. issue in Aug. 1981 and Jan. 1982.
4. Set includes revised editions of some issues.
5. Some vols. issued in revised editions.
6. Vols. for 1981-   called Revised.
7. Vol. 1, revised and corrected, issued June 1975.
8. Vol. for 1978 issued in a revised ed., Aug. 1979.
9. Vols. for FY 1982 issued in 2 sets, the second being a revised edition.
10. Subsequent issues of each vol. constitute revisions of previous ones, which they supersede.
11. Issued in alternating Japanese and European editions with even no. being Japanese and describing Japanese cars and the odd no. being European, describing European cars.

F. Cumulations*
    1. Each vol. cumulates from 1909.
    2. Jan. issue is cumulative.
    3. Each issue is cumulative.
    4. Every 3rd issue is a quarterly cumulation.
    5. One issue per month cumulates previous month's weekly issues.
    6. Vol. 1-3, no. 2 superseded by a cumulative issue.
    7. Each issue cumulative from the Jan. issue.
    8. Vols. for   -1977/80 are cumulative.
    9. Only cumulative annual issue published for 1980.
    10. Each issue cumulates the preceding year for a period of up to five years.
    11. Dec. issue each year is a cumulation of prior issues.
    12. Dec. vol. for 1982-   is cumulative for the year.
    13. The June issue, called 1. Halbjahr, cumulates Jan.-May; the Dec. issue, called Jahresband, cumulates Jan.-Nov.
    14. Cumulates the abstracts and indexes originally published in monthly issues Jan.-Dec., generally covering publications issued Oct.-Sept.

VI. PRELIMINARY ISSUES

1. Charter issue published in 1978.
2. Pre-publication issue published July 1980.
3. An introductory number was issued as Test number 0-1978.
4. Issue for Jan. 1982 called also premier issue.
5. Issue for spring 1982, called also "Premier issue," lacks numbering but constitutes v. 1, no. 1.
6. Vol. 1, no. 1 preceded by three "experimental issues."
7. Unnumbered vol. titled: Logic and data bases, constitutes v. 0.
8. A "prototype issue" called v. 1, no. 0 was issued Oct. 16, 1978.
9. Vol. 1, no. 1 preceded by unnumbered, undated prototype issue.
10. Preceded by a proposed newsletter dated Dec. 1981.
11. Vol. 1, no. 1, preceded by an issue numbered v. 1, no. 1 and called: Prospectus 1968.
12. Vol. 1, no. 1 preceded by a number dated Dec. 1965 called Subscription issue.

---

*For cumulations issued under separate title, see "580 Linking Entry Complexity Note."

13. Vol. 1, no.1 preceded by a number dated July/Dec.
1975, and a transitional volume dated May 1973-
June 1975.
14. Vol. 1, no. 1 preceded by a sample issue called also v. 1,
no. 1 and dated Nov. 15, 1977.
15. Vol. 0, published 1972, covers periodical literature
published from 1954 until the issuance of v. 1 in
1964.

VII. SUSPENSION OF PUBLICATION

1. Suspended 1974-1976.
2. Publication was suspended from Nov. 15, 1838-Jan. 1,
1839 when last number appeared.
3. Suspended with v. 10, 1917 and resumed with New ser.,
v. 1 (Dec. 1924).
4. Suspended following its May 1969 issue.   Resumed with
Jan. 1970 issue.
5. Publication was temporarily suspended with no. 2, May-
June 1963; resumed with July 1966 issue.
6. Suspended 1962-1972; a four volume set covering 1962-
1972 was published in 1976.

VIII. ITEMS NOT PUBLISHED

1. None published 1974.
2. No issue published for 1979.
3. Not published Mar.-Dec. 1973.
4. No separate issue published for 1977-1978.
5. No numbers issued for Sept. 1914-July 1915 and 1944.
6. No conference records published before 1978.
7. No proceedings published for the first 5 conferences.
8. Proceedings of the 1st-66th meetings not published.
9. No annuals published for 1940-1946? when the academy
was merged with the Accademia d'Italia.
10. Issues for 1948-1958 which constitute v. 26-34 not
published.
11. Vol. 1, Section F and all sections of June 1943 not
published.
12. No. 49-50 announced but never published.
13. Vols. 1-33 not published. Adopts its numbering from
Bulletin signalétique and its continuations.

Supplement Note

SCOPE

"Field 525 is used to clarify or amplify any supplement or special issue relationships that are not input as separate records. Generally, this field is used <u>only</u> for unnamed supplements and/or special issues." — OCLC *Serials Format,* 2nd ed.

ARRANGEMENT

   I. Unnamed Supplements

  II. Named Supplements (Not Published Separately)

 III. Special Issues

 IV. Updates

  V. Accompanying Information

525 SUPPLEMENT NOTE

I. UNNAMED SUPPLEMENTS

1. Has some supplements.
2. Has occasional supplements.
3. Some issues include supplements.
4. Some numbers issued with supplements.
5. Each vol. includes supplements to the previous years.
6. Includes occasional unnumbered supplements.
7. Includes occasional consecutively numbered supplementary issues.
8. Some supplements are unnumbered.
9. Includes supplements and extraordinary issues.
10. Unpaged supplements accompany some numbers.
11. Separately paged supplements accompany some numbers.
12. Statistical supplements accompany some reports.
13. Some issues contain supplements on special topics.
14. Supplements accompany v. 12-
15. Supplements accompany vols. for 1971 and 1973.
16. Vol. 5-   accompanied by supplements issued in alternate years.
17. Supplements issued at intervals of two months.
18. Supplements published every July and Jan.
19. Includes an annual supplement.
20. With annual supplements between editions.
21. Supplements issued between some editions.
22. Vols. for 1979-   accompanied by supplemental translation of the text, available in various languages.
23. Some issues accompanied by separately paged supplements and sections consisting principally of convention proceedings, and list of members and branch societies.
24. Issues for 1952-   accompanied by supplement containing summaries of each article in English, French, and German.
25. Vol. 3 is cumulative supplement to each edition.
26. Supplementary material published separately on microfiche.
27. Has separately issued support documents reproduced on microfiche.
28. IDF standards and documents issued as supplements.
29. Uncumulated abstracts and indices issued as supplements.
30. The issues for 1977 and 1978 constitute the first and second supplements to the 1976 issue.

31. Supplements have been issued since 1929 (Archives v. 7, no. 1) and bear parallel numbering to the "Cahiers" of the Archives.

II. NAMED SUPPLEMENTS (NOT PUBLISHED SEPARATELY)*

1. Supplements with title: TV supplement accompany each number.
2. Some issues accompanied by unnumbered "Sonderheft."
3. Index for v. 1-20 (1947-66) also called its Supplementary publication, no. 3.
4. Separately paged supplements called Section 2 with title Trends and patterns accompany each number.
5. Vols. for 195 -19   accompanied by a supplementary report, dated July, with title: The midyear economic report.
6. First ed. accompanied by 2 supplements: suppl. 1, Additions, revisions, and labor unions; suppl. 2, Functional and topical listings.
7. No. 12 (July 1980) has a supplement dated July 1981 and called Research series, supplement.

III. SPECIAL ISSUES

1. Some volumes have a special issue.
2. Special issue published Sept. 1975.
3. Special issues accompany some no.
4. Special issues and annual booking editions issued as numbers of some volumes.
5. Some issues appear as special editions.
6. Some numbers are published as Monograph/special issues.
7. Some issues have no vol. numbering, but are called Special issue.
8. Accompanied by special issues devoted to conferences.
9. An industry reference guide is published annually as part of the publishing frequency of Landscape & turf industry.
10. Includes an annual July 15 issue with title: Buyer's guide directory issue.

---

*For named supplements published separately, see "580 Linking Entry Complexity Note."

11. Includes an annual Handbook issue (safety regulations) pub. mid-Mar.; Energy equipment planning guide (varies) pub. in mid-July.

IV. UPDATES*

1. Kept up-to-date by irregular supplements.
2. Kept up-to-date by cumulative supplements.
3. Editions kept up-to-date by midyear supplements.
4. Quarterly updating supplements are issued between editions.
5. Updating supplements issued quarterly during 1973.
6. Updating supplements published April, July, and October.
7. Kept up-to-date with supplemental sheets.
8. Updated by continuing supplementary material and cumulated irregularly.
9. Kept up-to-date by supplementary bulletins issued twice monthly.
10. Updated by irregular supplements which are combined annually with cumulative indexes.
11. Vols. for 1976/77-   updated by biennial Bibliography supplement.
12. Vols. for 1981-   kept up-to-date by semiannual supplements.
13. Vols. for 1981-   kept up-to-date with an annual cross-referenced supplement.
14. Kept up-to-date 1963-1972 by semi-annual supplements covering all pts.; from 1973-   each pt. is kept up-to-date by a cumulated supplement.
15. Updates issued from time to time are called supplements.
16. Kept up-to-date by supplement issued for the year intervening between biennial publication.
17. Kept up-to-date by annual supplements which augment, but do not replace, main volume.
18. Monthly issues are in the form of supplements which partially update two main volumes.

V. ACCOMPANYING INFORMATION

1. Some issues accompanied by preliminary data.
2. Addendum accompany some numbers.

---

*For updates that are not supplements, see "500 General Note"; for named updates, see "580 Linking Entry Complexity Note."

3. First biennial report provides an overview.   A more detailed document issued as an Addendum.
4. Technical appendixes accompany some numbers.
5. Accompanied each year by separate reports on various areas.
6. Vols. for 1981-   are accompanied by two vols. that contain commissioned materials.
7. Vols. for 1981-   accompanied by narrative statements of federal courts in separately published appendices.
8. Accompanied by loose-leaf vol. containing current decisions and index.
9. Accompanied by separately issued vol. for table of contents titled sōmokuji, each covering 5 vols. in 5 years.
10. Second ed. accompanied by a geographic index.
11. Vols. for   contain index matrix (35 x 27 cm. folded to 18 x 14 cm.).
12. Vols. for   accompanied by map, in pocket.
13. Vols. for   accompanied by folded color map.
14. Col. map (laid in) accompanies every volume.
15. No. 25-26 accompanied by sound disc.
16. Issue for Sept. 1980 accompanied by sound recording.
17. Microfiche in pockets.
18. New ser., v. 1, no. 1-   contain sound disc (33⅓ rpm ; ser., 7 in.).

530
Additional Physical Forms
Available Note

SCOPE

"Field 530 is used when a serial published in one form is also generally available in other media. For example, ALA Bulletin was originally issued in print but is also available on microfilm from University Microfilms. Each form is cataloged separately, and the record for each form may contain a note describing the other form(s).

If the publisher of a serial in another physical form is different from the original publisher, the name of the publisher of the other form is also noted.

If the work is a reprint (regular, eye-readable print), use field 260 for reprint information and describe the original work in field 580." — OCLC *Serials Format*, 2nd ed.

530 ADDITIONAL PHYSICAL FORMS AVAILABLE NOTE

1. Available in current microfiche ed.
2. Also issued on microfiche.
3. Issued also on microfilm from University Microfilms.
4. Issued also on microfiche simultaneously with the paper edition on microfilm at end of subscription year.
5. Available on microfilm from Xerox University Microfilms.
6. Available on microfilm from Johnson Associates, Inc., University Microfilms, and Princeton Microfilms.
7. Also available in 16-millimeter microfilm.
8. Available also in microfiche, which includes supplementary material.
9. Vols. for   distributed to depository libraries in microfiche.

34

533
Photoreproduction Note

SCOPE

"For the cataloging of microreproductions and certain macroreproductions, the Library of Congress bases the bibliographic description on the original publication and describes the reproduction in a note. Field 533 contains the note describing the reproduction." — OCLC *Serials Format,* 2nd ed.

1. Vol. 2-   photocopy.   Nendeln, Liechtenstein : Kraus Reprint,   1967-   24 cm.
2. Microfilm.   Ann Arbor, Mich. : Xerox University Microfilms, microfilm reels ; 35 mm. (Current periodical series).
3. Microfiche.   Cambridge, England : Chadwyck-Healey Ltd. ; Teaneck, N.J. : Somerset House, 1977. microfiche sheets ; 10 x 15 cm. (European official statistical serials on microfiche).
4. Microfiche.   Ann Arbor, Mich. : University Microfilms International, 1979-   sheets ; 11 x 15 cm. (Current periodical series ; pub. no. 2203.).

546

Language Note

SCOPE

"Field 546 contains a note concerning languages of the text." — OCLC *Serials Format*, 2nd ed.

ARRANGEMENT

  I. Language of Text

 II. Summary Information

III. Translation Information

546   LANGUAGE NOTE

I.   LANGUAGE OF TEXT*

1. Papers published in any language.
2. Text is multilingual (romanized).
3. Each issue in various European languages.
4. Articles are in English, French, German, Italian, Portuguese, etc.
5. Entries in English and Chinese.
6. Titles cited in original language with translation in English.
7. Text in English, German, and other languages.
8. Chinese, 1978-   , English, 1976-   , and Portuguese.
9. French, Mar./June 1981-   ; Dutch and French,
10. Text in English only.
      [Parallel titles in English and French]
11. Text in English; comparative tables in English and French.
12. Title and text in Danish, Dutch, English, French, German and Italian; title also in Greek.
13. Annotations in French and English.
14. Includes some text in French.
15. Chiefly in English; some also in French and German.
16. Chiefly in Italian with occasional contributions in German.
17. Text in English; includes some textual material in other European languages.
18. Articles primarily in Dutch, some in English.
19. In French or in various other languages with French translation.
20. Title also in French, Italian, and Dutch; text in French and English with glossary and table of contents in English, Danish, Dutch, French, German, and Italian.
21. Text in English and French in parallel columns.
22. In English and French, with French text on inverted pages.
23. Text in English and French, 1971-   ; French text on inverted pages, 1976/77-
24. Reports for the years   have parallel texts in German and English.
25. Text in English and French, each with special t.p. and separate paging. French text on inverted pages.
26. No. 1-5 contain parallel texts in French and English; no. 6-   available in either English or French editions.

---

*For notes concerning language of title/parallel title information, see "500 General Note."

27. Publication available in German, French and/or English.
No. 22-   has title only in the language of
the text.
28. Vol. for Sept. 1967 published entirely in English.

II. SUMMARY INFORMATION

1. Some summaries in English and French.
2. In English with summaries in French.
3. Text in German and English; English summaries.
4. English text; summaries in Spanish, Russian, and Polish.
5. In Chinese and Japanese; with summaries in Chinese, English, and Japanese.
6. Early issues include English and French summaries of selected articles.
7. Articles in English, French, and German; summaries in all three languages.
8. Text in Dutch and English, the former with summaries in English.
9. In Turkish and English; each article accompanied by a summary in the other language.
10. Articles in English and French with summaries in the alternate langauge.
11. Articles in French and English with summaries in one or both of these languages.
12. English and French, with summaries in the other language and in Spanish or German.
13. Portuguese, with some articles in English; summaries in English and French.
14. Text in German and French; tables of contents also in Polish and Russian; summaries in Polish and Russian.
15. Articles largely in Japanese, some in English; some tables of contents and summaries in English.
16. Articles mainly in English with some in French and Italian; summaries in English, French, German, Italian, and Spanish.
17. German articles with summaries or abstracts in English; English articles with summaries or abstracts in German; some French.
18. Tables of contents also in French; summaries in French and English.
19. Some vols. are accompanied by a separately paged summary in French and English.

III.   TRANSLATION INFORMATION*

1. In Portuguese, with the second half of the issue being the English translation.
2. French translation of Chinese articles, with summaries in English and French.
3. Multilingual; foreign language contributions usually with English translation.

---

*For general translation information, see "500 General Note."

550
Issuing Bodies Note

SCOPE

"Field 550 is used for notes referring to issuing bodies, including official organ notes and notes that contain editing, compiling, or translating information involving an issuing body.

Publishers that can be considered corporate bodies are named in a 550 note, with added entries in field 710 or 711."—OCLC *Serials Format,* 2nd ed.

ARRANGEMENT

  I. General Issuing Body Notes

 II. Publisher Information

III. Official Organ, Publication, etc.

VI. Variant Names

550   ISSUING BODIES NOTE

I.   GENERAL ISSUING BODY NOTES

1. Issued by: Pennsylvania State Library, Oct. 1963-Mar. 1971; State Library of Pennsylvania, 1972-
2. Earlier vols. issued by Alabama Dept. of Public Health, Special Services Administration, Division of Vital Statistics.
   [Description based on: 1980]
3. Issued by a committee comprised of various French governmental agencies.
4. Second quarter 1979-   issued jointly with Bureau of Industrial Economics.
5. Vol. for 1979 issued with: Oficina de Planificación Agricola.
6. Sponsored by Region 5 of the Institute of Electrical and Electronics Engineers, 1976; and by other sections of the Institute, 1977-
7. Institutes sponsored by the American Chemistry Society and the Royal Chemistry Society.
8. No. 2-3 (May 1981)-   sponsored jointly by the International Funds for the Promotion of Culture of UNESCO and by EACROTANAL.
9. Developed by: the Library, and Information Services Division, Environmental Science Information Center.
10. Proceedings compiled by the ARC Weed Research Organization.
11. Compiled and edited by the Cataloging Publication Division, Library of Congress.
12. 2nd-   report prepared by the Dept.'s Bureau of Automotive Repair.
13. Prepared for the annual meeting with the assistance and cooperation of the Gulf Coast Section of the Society of Economic Paleontologists and Mineralogists, 1954-
14. Individual issues prepared in cooperation with various local agencies.
15. Produced by: students at San Diego State University.
16. Produced in cooperation with Burwood State College.
17. Measured in cooperation with: the Arkansas Geological Commission.
18. Founded by the Central Ontario Industrial Relations Institute and now published in cooperation with the Office of Arbitration, Ontario Ministry of Labour.
19. Report submitted by the Commissioner of Teachers' Pensions.

20. Vols. for   -1980 approved by the World Food and
    Agricultural Outlook and Situation Board.
21. Translated by: Mainichi Daily News,   -1979; Japan
    Times, Ltd., 1980-
22. Made possible by a grant from the Lederle Laboratories.
23. Automated rights held by Fandom Computer Services.

II. PUBLISHER INFORMATION*

1. Published by chemical societies in Denmark, Finland,
   Norway, and Sweden.
2. Published as a trial research project by the Program
   Evaluation Resource Center.
3. Vols. for 1965-19   published by Asian Peoples' Anti-
   Communist League.
   [Imprint: [Taipei : s.n., 1965?-   ]
4. Vol. 2 and alternate vols. thereafter published in Wrochaw
   by Państwowe Wydawn. Naukowe.
5. Published by the Music Section of the Department of
   Cultural Affairs of the Pan American Union, to
   complement the more extensive Boletín interameri-
   cano de Música published by the Section in Spanish.
6. Chinese language edition for foreign distribution published
   by Hsiang-kang hsien tai wen hua ch'i yeh kung ssu;
   original domestic edition by Ching chi kuan li tsa chih
   she, 1981-
7. No. 1 (fall 1970)-   published in association with Stony
   Brook Poetics Foundation; New ser., v. 1, no. 1-v. 4, no.
   2 published by Boston University.
8. Published under the auspices of the Rutgers Institute
   of Jazz Studies, 1982-
9. Published under the auspices of: Gesellschaft Deutscher
   Chemiker, Deutsche Gesellschaft für Chemisches
   Apparatewesen, VDI-Gesellschaft Verfahrenstechnik
   und Chemieingenieurwesen (GVC).
10. Some numbers also published by Colorado Dept. of
    Health.
11. Published with the support of the International Association
    of Hotel Management Schools.
12. Quarterly publication of the Salnaker Family Association,
    Oct. 1979-

---

*For imprint variation notes, see "500 General Note."

13. Published for the International Society for Test Anxiety Research, 1982-
14. Published on behalf of the Faculty of Law, University of Oxford, spring 1981-

III. OFFICIAL ORGAN, PUBLICATION, ETC.

1. Official organ of the American Institute of Architects, San Francisco chapter and other local chapters, 19   -Aug. 1918.
2. Official organ of: the Imperial Society of Teachers of Dancing (with which the Cecchetti Society is incorporated), Oct. 1925-Sept. 1939.
3. Official journal of: Foust Industry Engineering Association and the Timber Machinists Educational Association.
4. Official magazine of the Southern Rhodesia Tourist Board, July/Aug. 1964-Sept./Oct. 1964; of Rhodesia National Tourist Board, Nov./Dec. 1964-Mar./Apr. 1965.
5. Official publication of the National Society for Performance and Instruction.
6. Beginning with Jan. 1941, issued as the bulletin of the Société de géographie.
7. With the May 1976 issue it became the official organ of: the Australian Apple and Pear Corporation, and: the Australian Apple and Pear Growers Association. Their official notes appear in a special supplement: Apple and pear world, in the center section of the journal each month.
8. Issued also as the journal of the Surveyors Institute of Zambia, Mar. 1979-

IV. VARIANT NAMES

1. Issued by the bank under its English form of name: National Bank of Ethiopia, 1964-
2. Vols. for   issued under a variant English name: Institute of Developing Economies.
   [Imprint: Institute of Asian Economic Affairs]
3. No. 1 issued by the foundation under its variant form of name: Foundation for Australian Studies.
   [Uniform title: Monograph (Foundation for Australian Literary Studies)]
4. Issues for Nov. 1942-Dec. 1942 published by the center under a different name: United Nations Information Office.

5. Prior to Mar. 1978 issued by the Service under its earlier name: United States. Environmental Data Service.
6. Vols. for Jan. 1979-   issued under the Office of Administration's new name, the Office of Management and Agency Services.
7. Issued 1975-1977 by Research Section, Dept. of Health and Social Development (called 1978-1979, Dept. of Health and Community Services).
   [Imprint: Winnipeg? : Research and Program Planning, Manitoba Dept. of Health,   ]
8. Issuing body varies slightly: Skipjack Programme.
   [Title: Skipjack Survey and Assessment Programme]

555
Cumulative Index
Note/Finding Aids

SCOPE

"Field 555 contains a statement of volumes and/or dates covered by cumulative indexes and also the location of those indexes (whether issued as part of the serial or issued separately)." — OCLC *Serials Format*, 2nd ed.

ARRANGEMENT

I. Tabular Notes

II. Informal Notes

555   CUMULATIVE INDEX NOTE/FINDING AIDS*

I.   TABULAR NOTES

1.   Vols. 1 (1958)-5 (1962) with v. 5.
     Vols. 1 (1958)-10 (1967) with v. 10.
2.   Vols. 1 (1961)-4 (1966) in v. 4 of: Columbia journal of
     transnational law.
3.   Vol. 2, no. 2 (1968)-v. 5, no. 1 (spring 1970) in the Journal
     of international law and economics, v. 9, no. 3 (1974).
4.   Vols. 1 (1843/49)-20 (1899) issued as v. 21, pt. 1.   1 v.
     Vols. 21 (1900)-40 (1920) in v. 44.
     Vols. 21 (1900)-60 (1940) issued as American Oriental series,
     v. 40.   1 v.
5.   Vols. 1 (1967)-11 (1978) with v. 11 (Includes index to the
     periodical under its earlier title).
6.   Vols. 1 (1969)-3 (1971) with v. 3 (Includes index to the journal
     under its earlier name).
7.   Vols. 2 (1926)-10 (1935) in v. 10 of later title.
8.   Vols. 1 (1959)-10 (1968) (Includes index to journal under
     its earlier and later titles).
9.   1912-1957.   1 v.   (Includes index to journal under its
     earlier and later titles.)
10. Tenth year index: 1973-1982.   1 v.   (Includes v. 1-3 of
     Poetry nation, no. 1-8 of PN review, and no. 9 of Poetry
     nation review.)
11. Vols. 1 (1849)-58 (1907). 1 v. (Includes indexes to the
     association's earlier proceedings and transactions
     under the name of Indiana State Medical Society.)
12. Author indexes:
     Issues 1 (1966)-12 (1970).   1 v.
     Issues 13 (1971)-24 (1974).   1 v.
     Issues 25 (1975)-36 (1979).   1 v.
13. Author index:
     Vol. 1 (1976)-   with v. 2-
     Subject index:
     Vol. 1 (1976)-   with v. 2-

---

*Notes in this chapter are listed as they would appear on the catalog card, with the
exception that the word "Indexes" which would normally begin each note has been
omitted. For instructions on inputting the 555 field, see the OCLC *Serials Format.*

II.   INFORMAL NOTES

1. Includes decennial indexes.
2. Annual index in latter issues.
3. Vol. 118 is index to v. 87-117.
4. Annual author and subject indexes.
5. Complete title, subject, and author index published on a 5-issue and 10-issue basis.
6. Subject indexes, cumulative from 1964, included in vols. for 1965-
7. Each vol. includes cumulative index to preceding vols.
8. Beginning with 17, each issue contains a cumulative author index.
9. The last vol. for each session is (or includes) a general index for the vols. in that session.
10. Index of contents, v. 1 (1961)-16 (1974) published separately in 1975.
11. Index published separately each year.
12. Each issue contains cumulative index to all issues.
13. Index to ASTM standards issued as last part of each vol.
14. Cumulative indexes published semi-annually; 1980- one semiannual index issued for Jan.-June.
15. Vol. 53, no. 4 constitutes cumulative index to Inland bird banding and the titles which preceded it.
16. With the 1979 edition a cumulated index covering the documents lists 1975-1979 has been produced.
17. Index for FY 73-FY 80, published in 1 vol., also covers serial under its earlier title: Federal program evaluations.

580
Linking Entry
Complexity Note

SCOPE

"Field 580 is used for free text notes expressing complex relationships with other publications. Use field 580 when an intelligible note cannot be generated using the print constants associated with linking entry fields 780 and 785, or could not be generated if linking entry fields 760-777, 787 were printing fields. Whenever a note is entered in field 580, the entry(ies) of the related publication(s) must also be entered in the appropriate linking field(s).

If the work is a reprint, use field 260 for reprint information and describe the original work in field 580." — OCLC *Serials Format,* 2nd ed.

ARRANGEMENT

   I. General Linking Notes
- A. Absorptions
- B. Continuations
- C. Mergers
- D. Miscellaneous general linking notes

  II. Cumulations, Summaries, etc.

 III. Editions
- A. Language
- B. Miscellaneous edition information

 IV. Previously published elsewhere
- A. Reprints
- B. Miscellaneous previous publication notes

  V. Specific and Nonspecific Relationships
- A. Specific number(s) or issue(s)
- B. Nonspecific number(s) or issue(s)

580 LINKING ENTRY COMPLEXITY NOTE

I. GENERAL LINKING NOTES

A. Absorptions
1. Absorbed by: Scott stamp monthly, as a separately numbered section Nov. 1983.
2. Absorbed: Crystal structure communications, and assumed the numbering of the other sections of Acta crystallographica.
3. Absorbed: Erdöl und Teer (1 (1925)-10 (1934)) in 1935 and continued its numbering until Sept. 1939.
4. Absorbed: The Inspector, May 1927; California southland, Feb. 1929; and: California home owner, May 1929.
5. Following absorption of Metalworking news, Monday issue called American metal market, Metalworking news edition.
6. Beginning with new ser. v. 12 (July 1952) incorporates the Bibliography of industrial diamond applications which continues its own vol. numbering, v. 9, etc.
7. "Incorporating World list of scientific periodicals," which still appears as Cumulative annual volume of scientific titles.

B. Continuations
1. Continued in 1979 by: Members' handbook (Nairobi, Kenya).
2. Continued in part by: Journal of geophysical research. Oceans; and: Journal of geophysical research. Atmospheres.
3. Continued by a monographic series with the same title.
4. "Letters to the Editor" section continued as: Journal of materials science letters.
5. Beginning with v. 23, information on anthropological matter continued in: Anthropological papers of the American Museum of Natural History.
6. Alternate issues for Sept. 1970-July 1977 published in "newsletter format," continued separately Aug. 1977-   as: NARD newsletter, ISSN 0162-1602.
7. Product directory section continued by: ASHRAE product specification file, which accompanies each volume of ASHRAE handbook.
8. Called New series in continuation of: Acta embryologiae experimentalis.

9. Continues: Law book guide (New York, N.Y.), ISSN 0146-3861, published by Computext Communications, Ltd., and Law book guide, ISSN 0000-0353, a cumulated edition published by G.K. Hall.
10. Continues: Arid lands abstracts, ISSN 0143-6368, published 1972-   with a different numbering designation.
11. Continues v. 3 of: United States. Energy Information Administration. Annual report to Congress, ISSN 0161-5807.
12. Continues the first section of the 11th edition of American men of science: a biographical directory.
13. Continues a bimonthly publication with the same title issued 19   -1966.
14. Continues the publication with the same title issued by the bureau when it was a part of the University of Hawaii.
15. Continues: 1001 decorating ideas (New York, N.Y.), ISSN 0030-2554.
16. Continues the supplements to: Monthly vital statistics report.
17. Continues the monthly issues, Jan.-Nov., of: International Monetary Fund. Balance of payments yearbook.
18. With similar titles, continues: Proceedings of the American Society of Civil Engineers.
19. With twelve or more similar titles, continues: Statistical register of Western Australia.
20. Future narrative sections of annual report will be included in an issue of CTA quarterly each year.
    [Annual title has ceased]
21. Continues the separate language editions: Assignment children; Les Carnets de l'enfance; and: Die Kinder dieser Welt, and continues their vol. numbering.

C. Mergers
    1. Merger of: New scientist; and: Science journal, and continues the numbering of the former.
    2. Merger of: ECS; and in part: Proceedings of the Institution of Electrical Engineers.
    3. Merger of: Étude (Philadelphia, Pa.); and: Musical world (Cleveland, Ohio), and continues the vol. numbering of the former.
    4. Merged with: Social science & medicine. Part A, Medical sociology; Social science & medicine. Part B, Medical anthropology; Social science & medicine. Part C, Medical economics; Social science & medicine. Part D, Medical geography; and: Social science & medicine. Part F, Medical & social ethics, to form: Social science & medicine (1982).

5. Formed by the union of: Acta geobotanica Barcinonensia, and: Acta phytotaxonomica Barcinonensia, and assumes numbering of the sum of their issues.

D. Miscellaneous general linking notes
    1. Issued 1964-1981 in two parts: Annales de paléontologie. Invertébrés, ISSN 0570-1619, and: Annales de paléontologie. Vertébrés, ISSN 0570-1627; changed back to: Annales de paléontologie with 1982.
    2. Separated from v. 2 of: Secured transactions in personal property in Canada by Richard H. McLaren, issued in loose-leaf format.
    3. Split into several subseries under the common title: Garcia de Orta.

II. CUMULATIONS, SUMMARIES, ETC.*

1. Cumulated annually on microfiche.
    [Annual title: Serials in the British Library (Annual)]
2. Cumulated annually with title: National Institutes of Health consensus development conference summaries.
3. Cumulates the monthly publication.
    [Uniform title: British technology index (Annual)]
4. Cumulates listings in quarterly paper issues of the same title.
5. Cumulation of a quarterly publication.
6. Cumulation of the quarterly publication with the same title.
7. Cumulation of the annual publication.
8. Cumulation of a bimonthly publication with the same title.
9. Annual cumulation of the weekly and its 4 cumulated bulletins.
10. A cumulation of the citations which appeared during 1977-1978 in: Biogenic amines and transmitters in the nervous system, ISSN 0006-3077.
11. Also issued in annual cumulation.

---

*For cumulations not issued as separate titles, see "515 Numbering Peculiarities Note."

12. Issued also in an annual cumulation called: Telegen reporter review.
13. Issued also in irregular cumulations and called: Economics selections.
14. Cumulations are issued under the title: The Gramophone popular record catalogue. Master edition.
15. Title of annual cumulation varies slightly: Bell & Howell's newspaper index. Washington post.
16. Data were cumulated quinquennially in: Surface water supply of the United States.
17. Quinquennial cumulations issued as vols. of the quinquennial cumulations of: National Union Catalog, ISSN 0028-0348.
18. Combines all non-duplicative elements of: Overseas business reports.
19. Quarterly summaries of the data and other information significant to the area are published in: Labor market bulletin.
20. Compilation of the monthly publication: Insider newsletter.
21. Summary of the monthly publication: Direction of trade statistics.
22. Each issue represents a computerized search of 2 consecutive odd issues of: Chemical abstracts.
23. Each issue represents an exhaustive computerized search of 6 consecutive issues of: Chemical abstracts.
24. Publication is a condensation of pertinent gas industry statistics adapted from: Gas facts.
25. Replaces the annual paperback compilations of: Index Islamicus. Supplement, and will be cumulated by its quinquennial supplements.
26. The 12 monthly reports for a fiscal year are tabulated and published as: Preliminary national annual medicaid statistics, which are then compiled as: National annual medicaid statistics.

III. EDITIONS

A. Language
1. Also published in French ed.
2. Issued also in an English ed., 1955-1966.
3. Issued also in Russian and v. 2-   in English.
4. Published also in German and Spanish eds.
5. Also published in English ed. with the same title.
6. Also published in French under title: Sommaire des communications, ISSN 0226-7489.

7. Other editions available: Au courant (Economic Council of Canada. Communications Division). French.
8. Arabic ed. of: Arab Bank for Economic Development in Africa. Annual report.

B. Miscellaneous edition information
1. Appears in both print and braille editions.
2. Issued also in a quadrennial edition.
3. Issued in four editions: Central ed., Eastern ed., Southern ed., Western ed.,   ; in various regional commodity editions,
4. Expanded companion ed. of: Information Moscow.
5. Issued in Australia as: Geo; outside Australia as: Journey.
6. Published as: Information trade directory, ISSN 0142-0208, outside North and South America.
7. Beginning in 1955 another ed. is published in Tübingen with different editors and contents but which assumes the vol. numbering of the Halle ed.
8. Special premium ed. issued 1979-80: The Hammond almanac.

IV. PREVIOUSLY PUBLISHED ELSEWHERE

A. Reprints
1. Reprint.   Originally published quarterly: New York, N.Y. : The Armchair Detective, Inc.
2. Reprint of an annual published in Berlin.
3. Reprint of the Aug. issue of: Art in America.
4. Reprint of the publication with the same title.
5. Reprint of: Working paper series, no. 1 (1974)-   published individually by the Academy.
6. Reprint, with an introduction.   Originally published biweekly (irregular): Lima : [s.n.].
7. Reprint, with an introduction.   Originally published monthly: México : Escuela Normal Primaria para Maestros.
8. Reprint, with an introduction, of a monthly periodical published in Mexico.
9. Reprint, with an introduction, of a periodical published 1928-
10. Reprint, with an introduction added, of a periodical published in Cambridge, Mass., Bronx, New York, and San Francisco.
11. Reprint, with introduction and new material added, of a newsletter published in New York and edited by D. Di Prima, 1961-1969 (with L. Jones, 1961-1962).

12. Reprint, with two supplements added: Dav a censúra, and Bibliografia "Davu". Originally published irregularly: Praha : 'L. Obtulovič, 1924-1925; Bratislava : Zd. Merc (varies), 1926-1937. Issues for 1926-1936 called also v. 2-v. 8. Suspended 1927-1928.
13. Reprint ed. published with introduction and author-title alphabetical index.
14. Reprinted with: Escala (Mexico City, Mexico), t. 1, no. 1 (oct. de 1930)-t. 1, no. 2 (nov. de 1930).
15. Contains collected reprints of articles from: Parasitology.
16. Contents reprinted from: AIA journal.
17. Expanded and edited papers selected from: Ti ch'iu hua hsüeh.
18. Most no. are reprinted from Circulation or Circulation research.
19. Selected articles are reprinted in: Readings in Gulf Coast geology.
20. Vol. 1 is a reissue of: Etudes géographiques, 1re année, fasc. 1 (janv. 1900)-1re année, fasc. 4 (oct. 1900).
21. Vol. 1 is a revised and reprinted ed. of the Kansas working papers in anthropology and linguistics, 1976.
22. Vol. 1, no. 1 is a reprint of v. 1, no. 1 of the New York Law School International Law Society journal.
23. Vol. 1, no. 1 of Cousins et cousines is a reprint of v. 1, no. 1 of: Digging for roots.
24. Vol. 1, no. 1 (fall 1970) is a reprint of all previous issues of the Memphis State University law commentary.
25. Vol. for 1960 is a reprint of no. 1-6, Feb.-Dec. 1960 which were issued jointly with: Communications of ACM, ISSN 0001-0782.
26. Vols. for 1909-1911 reprinted from the Annual report of the American Historical Association; 1918-1929 issued as supplement to the report; 1930-1931, 1935- issued as v. 2 of the report; 1932, as v. 3; and 1933-1934 as the complete report.

B. Miscellaneous previous publication notes
   1. Contains updated articles published 1977-   in: MICRO.
   2. Consists of cases originally reported in: Copyright law reporter.
   3. Includes information previously presented in: Weekly coal production; and in: Coal distribution.
   4. Previously published in 1978 as: Directory of federal regional structure.

5. Earlier information in: The Literature of American history, and its supplements.
6. Earlier reports issued by the Service under its earlier name, Legislative Reference Service, as part of the Annual report of the Librarian of Congress.
7. Earlier vols. issued as part of: City finances.
8. Similar information formerly included in: Centro International de Agricultura Tropical. Annual report.
9. Previously published as a separately paginated section in: Water & sewage works.
10. Previously published as separate reports.
11. Previously published as part of: Regnum Vegetabile.
12. Previously issued in: Il Nuovo cimento, under title: Lettere alla redazione.
13. Formerly issued as a supplement to: Landscape & turf.
14. Formerly issued as a section of: Directory, home centers & hardware chains, auto supply chains.
15. Beginning in 1950, contains separately paged sections previously published separately: In Jewish bookland, Jewish music notes, and Jewish bookland, Oct. 1971-
16. Previously published as a section inserted in: AHA guide to the health care field of the American Hospital Association.
17. No. 1-49 originally appeared in a newspaper called the Craftsman. Beginning with no. 50 (Sept. 29, 1953), the last 52 no. were issued separately. When reprinted in 1956, the 101 no. were extended to 104 no. with alterations.
18. Through 1979 information was included in the regional editions of Financial assistance by geographic area issued by the Dept. of Health, Education, and Welfare, Office of the Deputy Assistant Secretary, Finance.
19. Includes Italian translations of articles originally published in: Biologie médicale (SPECIA Society).
20. Previously issued in the Society's Yearbook.
21. Reports for 1957-1975? included in Jan. issues of its Business review, third Federal reserve district.
22. Comprises, in tabular form, all of the information previously published in: Bulletin of the International Seismological Centre.
23. Groups together the methodological notes of all the statistics reproduced in OECD financial statistics, pts. 1-3.
24. Data for   extracted from: United States. Energy Information Administration. Annual report to Congress.
25. Report for 1894 extracted from: Das Recht der Frau.

26. Short-term energy projections provided by: Short-term energy outlook, ISSN 0270-8205.
27. Issues for July 1952-1964 accompanied by: Statistical supplement, formerly included in statistics section of Review, and was continued in 1965 by: Bulletin of labour statistics.
28. Prior to Aug. 1977, the newsletter was published as alternate issues of NARD journal.

V.   SPECIFIC AND NONSPECIFIC RELATIONSHIPS

A. Specific number(s) or issue(s)*
1. Annual June special issue of: Euromoney.
2. Issued annually as an unnumbered 4th issue of: Housing and society.
3. Published annually by: Training, as pt. 2 of the Aug. issue.
4. Some vols. issued as pt. 2 of one number of the Bulletin of the American Mathematical Society.
5. Vol. 1 published as a special issue of: The Jurist.
6. Issue for spring 1982 is a special section of: Landscape architecture.
7. Issued every 3 years as v. 2 of: Population programmes and projects.
8. Issued every July as the "Directory issue" of' Public relations journal.
9. Issue for 1979-   issued as special Nursing job guide issue of Nursing job news and dated Jan. 15.
10. Vols. for 1956-1968 issued as the Sept. number of the Journal of Asian studies.
11. Vols. for   issued as the Mar. number of: Soybean digest.
12. Vol. for 1972/73 published as Nov. issue of: American libraries.
13. Also issued as v. 49, no. 1-2 of: Revue de l'Université d'Ottawa.
14. The 2nd-3rd annual reports, 1916-1917, are found also in the 3rd-4th annual reports of the Federal Reserve Board, 1916-1917.

*For names of titles within a serial not issued separately, see "500 General Note."

15. Beginning with v. 48 (1954) issue no. 2 of each vol. issued as: Papers and proceedings of the American Economic Association.
16. No. 1-11 appeared as a section of: Kurtrierisches Jahrbuch, 1969-1979.
17. No. 4 of v. 22-27 issued as: Drake law review insurance law annual, called also: Insurance law annual.
18. Vol. 2 of the Annual report issued separately as: Merger decisions.

B. Nonspecific number(s) or issue(s)*
 1. Beginning with 1979 the Directory is issued as one of the quarterly issues of the Bulletin of the Association of Engineering Geologists.
 2. Issued as a number of: School business affairs, 19
 3. Published as an annual issue of: Industrial research & development.
 4. Issued as a section of: Journal of molecular structure, and included in its numbering also.
 5. Issued in: Childhood education, Sept./Oct. 1981-Nov./Dec. 1981.
 6. Published as an insert to accompany numerous Canadian newspapers.
 7. Vols. for Nov. 1982-Oct. 1983 issued as an insert to: Scott stamp monthly, with a limited number issued separately to dealers.
 8. Jan.-Feb. 1981-   published as part of: Macromolecular chemistry and physics.
 9. Vols. for   -1977/78 issued as part of the series: Gallup opinion index.
 10. A pullout section of: Advertising age.
 11. Special issue of: Apparel industry magazine.

C. Companion volumes
 1. Has a companion volume with title: Reverse acronyms, initialisms, & abbreviations dictionary, ISSN 0270-4390 (called v. 3).
 2. Vols. for 1976-   called v. 3, a companion volume to: Acronyms, initialisms, & abbreviations dictionary, ISSN 0270-4404.
 3. Complements: Collier on bankruptcy.
 4. Companion series to the journal: Studies in language.

---

*For names of titles within a serial not issued separately, see "500 General Note."

D. Indexes*
   1. Vols. 5 (1975)-   issued as the annual index to: Mathematical reviews, ISSN 0025-5629, v. 45 (1973)-
   2. Annual and cumulative index to: Government reports announcements & index, ISSN 0097-9007.
   3. Index to: Australian official journal of patents, trade marks, and designs.
   4. Indexes the microfiche collection: Curriculum development library.

E. Issued with
   1. Issued with: DA, Data Asia
      [Title: DA, West Asia report]
   2. Issued with and included in subscription to: Legal times.
   3. Vols. for 1981-   issued with: Wall street journal index.
   4. Vols. for 1963-   issued alternately with: Scientific and technical aerospace reports.
   5. Issued in alternating numbers with: Methodological surveys. A, Analysis.
   6. One no. a year issued jointly with: Yiddish, ISSN 0364-4308, and called 1977: Conference on Modern Jewish Studies annual, ISSN 0270-9392; called 1978-   : Modern Jewish studies annual, ISSN 0270-9406.

F. Supplements†
   1. Beginning in 1974, quarterly supplements continued by: Corporate action.
   2. English suppl. to the Journal of the Cerrahpaşa Medical Faculty.
   3. Issued as an annual supplement to: Nature.
   4. Vols. for 1980-   issued as supplement to: Industrie minérale.
   5. Issued as section 2 magazine supplement of: Back stage.
   6. Issued as supplement to National Book Centre of Pakistan. Books from Pakistan published during the decade of reforms, 1958-1968.
   7. A periodic supplement to: The Directory of directories.
   8. Supplement to accompany microfiche ed. of: Books in print.
   9. Supplement to, or in some years an issue of: Instrument manufacturing.

---

*For cumulative index notes, see "555 Cumulative Index Note/Finding Aids."

†For supplements not published separately, see "525 Supplement Note."

10. Vols. 1-3 issued as a supplement to Brain research; v. 4- to: Neuroscience.
11. Vols. for 19 -1977 issued as supplement to the Bulletin of the Association of Engineering Geologists.
12. Issues for 1946- contain unnumbered supplement: Schweisstechnik; later issued separately.
13. Vols. 1-4 include as a supplement a reprint of the Digital computer newsletter, v. 6 (1954)-9 (1957).
14. Vols. for 1981/82- issued as Supplement 2 to: The Book of the States.
15. Beginning with the 4th ed., a 3rd vol. (called New associations and projects (varies)) and, with the 18th ed. a 4th vol. (called International organizations) issued periodically in parts as inter-edition supplements.
16. In July 1934 American import export bulletin, ISSN 0002-886X, was established as a separate monthly publication to supplement the annual.

G. Updates*
1. Kept up-to-date between editions by: America buys. Updating service.
2. Kept up-to-date between editions by supplements appearing in: Foundation Center information quarterly, ISSN 0090-0524.
3. Kept up-to-date between editions by annual supplement: New acronyms, initialisms, and abbreviations, ISSN 0148-866X (called v. 2).
4. Kept up-to-date between editions by the biannual: Supplement to the directory of the American right, ISSN 0164-2510.
5. Kept up-to-date between volumes by: Monthly index to the Financial times.
6. Updated between editions by: Ernst & Whinney international quarterly.
7. Updated by: Law information update, a companion service issued ten times a year.
8. Designed to update the quarterly "Statistical indicators" bulletin.
9. Updates, with Corporate updates: Taft corporate directory.
10. Serves as an update to: Going public, by Robinson and Eppler.

---

*For unnamed updates, see "500 General Note"; for updates that are supplements, see "525 Supplement Note."

    11.   Vol. 1 of each ed. kept up-to-date by periodic supplement designated as v. 2, with title: New acronyms, initialisms & abbreviations.

H.   Miscellaneous specific and nonspecific relationship notes
    1.   Beginning with v. 10, no. 4, contents are the same as: Wage-price law and economics review, ISSN 0361-6665.
    2.   Contents identical with those of journal Ekonomska analiza, except that cover and contents page are in English.
    3.   Published concurrently by the U.S. Bureau of Industrial Economics under the title: Franchise opportunities handbook.
    4.   Published in association with Travel trade gazette.

VI. "INCLUDES" STATEMENTS*

1.   Includes: Datapro small computers news.
2.   Includes a separately numbered title: Monthly statement.
3.   Includes the annual Wine industry statistical report issued in different parts.
4.   Includes annual Micrographics equipment directory & buying guide as thirteenth issue, 1977-
5.   Issues for 1966-1975 of Sections A-C of the Transactions also include the Institution's separately numbered Bulletin, later published separately as: IMM bulletin, 1976-
6.   Issues include a separately paged insert entitled: World news examiner.
7.   Includes a separately paged section with the title: Pediatric infectious disease newsletter, v. 8, no. 1-
8.   Includes insert: Issuegram, winter 1982-
9.   Includes section with title: Vie académique, 1966-3 déc. 1973 (issued separately as a supplement beginning 10 déc. 1973).
10.   Includes unnumbered section called Library marketplace, which continues as independent publication.
11.   Includes a special number published in the summer of 1971 called "The Intrepid-Bear issue: Intrepid 20/ Floating Bear 38."

---

*For similar examples not connected to separately published titles, see "500 General Note."

12. Each issue includes sections: High fidelity (Great Barrington, Mass. : 1959), which is also issued separately, and: Musical America.
13. Most vols. include an issue called: Papers and proceedings of the Western Finance Association's annual meeting.
14. Vols. 13/14-   include: Povijest Dubrovnika, v. 2-
15. Vol. 1 (1967)-4 (1971) includes v. 12-16 of Metallurgical reviews.
16. Vols. for June 1982-   include: Updata, v. 12, no. 6 (June 1982)-
17. Issues for Nov. 9, 1981-   include a section called Creditwatch.   (Supplements to this section, with the same title, are periodically issued separately.)
18. Vol. for 1981 includes section 2 called: Electronics retailing, later issued separately.
19. Vols. for 1971-   include also: Annual report of the Division of Land Reclamation.
20. Vols. for 1962-   include alternate biennial revisions of: Current drug handbook, ISSN 0070-1939, also issued separately.
21. Vols. for 1956-1968 include Bibliography of Asian studies as the Sept. issue. Beginning with 1969 this bibliography is issued separately.
22. Vols. for 1964-   include section: American municipal news, previously issued as a separate publication.
23. Vols. for   include semi-annually: Designers west resource directory.
24. Vols. for   include the Harris Ohio buyers industrial directory, also issued separately.
25. Occasional issues, June 15, 1981-   include: ESF synchrotron radiation news, no. 6-   , issued by European Science Foundation, continuing European synchrotron radiation news.
26. Occasionally, timely economic data complementing the review is released in special issues called: U.S. long-term bulletin.
27. Beginning in Jan. 1977 issued in five parts, each part also published separately with individual vol. numbering: Cell physiology; Endocrinology, metabolism and gastrointestinal physiology; Heart and circulatory physiology; Regulatory, integrative and comparative physiology; Renal, fluid and electrolyte physiology.

28. The report of the Protective Department of the association (giving descriptions, portraits and facsimile signatures of forgers) forms a section of each vol., through v. 25, 1933/34; beginning with 1934/35 it appears separately under title: Protective bulletin, issued by the Protective Department of the American Bankers Association (numbered v. 27, etc., corresponding to the numbering of the American Bankers Association journal).
29. Some no. also published separately as: Documentary edition of American perfumer & aromatics.
30. Vols. 1-23/24 (1891/92-1914/15) include Bibliographie géographique annuelle (title varies) for 1891-1913/14, later issued separately and called 1931- Bibliographie géographique internationale.
31. Each issue also published in paperback with a distinctive title.
32. Section called "Phytopathology news" resumed independent publication in Sept. 1981.
33. Beginnng Sept. 28, 1960 each issue accompanied by: Science teacher's world.
34. Issues for 1945-1951 accompanied by War emergency issues (1950-1951 called W.E.P.) which constitute alternate vols. of the Proceedings, v. 153-165.
35. Vols. for Nov. 1982-Oct. 1983 accompanied by insert: Scott chronical of new issues.
36. Library vacancy roster and Roster of prospective federal librarians, and Guidelines for library handbooks issued as appendices.
37. Executive summary, foreword, introduction, categories of chemicals cataloged, and the Regulatory Council's statement on setting priorities for regulating carcinogens, for 1980- also issued separately as: Annual report on carcinogens. Executive summary.

VII. MISCELLANEOUS LINKING NOTES

1. All three sections of the Transactions are indexed in: Transactions. Contents, annual volume preliminary matter, name index, subject index.
2. Alternate biennial revisions for 1962/64- also included in: The Drug, the nurse, the patient.
3. Although the Journal incorporates the Transactions, annual vols. of selected papers are still continued in vols. uniform with the Transactions.

4. Abstracts from the first National Online Information Meeting, Mar. 25-27, 1980, were published as National Online Information Meeting: collected abstracts. Papers from that meeting were not published in the form of a proceedings volume.

5. A collection of contributions to: The American mercury (New York, N.Y. : 1924).

6. Each volume separately titled: v. 1, Acronyms, initialisms & abbreviations; v. 2, New acronyms, initialisms & abbreviations; v. 3, Reverse acronyms, initialisms & abbreviations dictionary.

7. Precedes the publication: U.S. lodging industry.

8. Prior to resumption of publication, an experimental vol. of the yearbook was issued in 1979 under the title: International guide to education systems.

9. Pub. also in Norfolk, Conn. by New Directions. [Other publication entitled: Orpheus (Norfolk, Conn.)]

10. Selected papers from the 1st annual meeting included in: Journal of the Atlantic Provinces Linguistic Association, ISSN 0706-6910.

11. Serves as advance sheets for Ohio State reports, Ohio Appellate reports, and Ohio Miscellaneous reports.

12. Statistics for 1949-1954 published in Sept. issue of the Social security bulletin, 1950-1955.

Sources

The following chapters contain information which will be helpful in locating the bibliographic record from which a particular note was taken. The source information is arranged to correspond with the tags and subsections found in the notes chapters.

The source entries include the title, Library of Congress card number (LCCN), and the OCLC record number when these numbers are available. For example:

	(Title)	(LCCN)	(OCLC)
1.	Artful dodge	sn80-134	#5872806

Blanks were left when either the number was unavailable or when the note was taken from the authors' original cataloging.

Please note that the notes which may have at one time appeared in the OCLC record may have been revised or deleted since we first searched the Online Union Catalog for the record number.

500   GENERAL NOTE

I.   INFORMAL SUMMARY/SCOPE NOTES

A.   Summary statements

1.	The As & Bs of academic scholarships	81-641778	#6162609
2.	Art serials	82-641866	#8286900
3.	C.S.I.R.O. abstracts	sc83-6022	#5257431
4.	Acta cartographica	68-7512	#1460858
5.	Bulletin (Sons of the Revolution. California Society : 1916)	sc82-6148	#8732810
6.	Hongkongiana	81-641464	#5629682
7.	Arkansas. State Board for Vocational Education. Arkansas annual plan for vocational education, PL94-482	83-640850	#5516335
8.	Songs on our way out	82-643842	#6186985
9.	Biennial report, human resources agencies	82-646457	#8541170
10.	Who's who in mass media	80-910501	#8436299
11.	Technical note (Forest Engineering Research Institute of Canada)	cn80-39014	#3418077

B.   General contents information

1.	American Society for Eighteenth Century Studies. ASECS directory		#2430286
2.	Unsere Kunstdenkmäler	sc82-3317	#2142005
3.	Media review	sn80-9192	#5934434
4.	Nordicom	79-646477	#4030466
5.	Hospital in-patient enquiry	83-641005	#4277923
6.	Cahiers d'études et de recherches victoriennes et édouardiennes	sn82-21358	#4031084
7.			
8.	Science resources studies highlights	sf83-1175	#3159753
9.	Courtauld Institute illustration archives. Archive 2, 15th & 16th century sculpture in Italy.		#3998337

10.	Woman poet (Reno, Nev.)	sn79-9109	#5526987
11.	Innovation (McLean, Va.)	82-643653	#8143097
12.	AMAA news	sc84-7471	#10411703
13.	Statistical report (Alaska. Division of Social Services)	83-640059	#9099738
14.	Serie separatas anuario	sn83-177	#7544443
15.	International yearbook of education	49-48323	#1753766

C. "Includes" statements

1.	Ohio official reports : new series : cases argued and determined in the courts of and in Ohio	sn82-5967	#8610029
2.	Bio-base	sn82-20513	#5214949
3.	Japon artistique	83-646228	#9987785
4.	The Musical mercury	sc83-7078	#9119421
5.	Bulletin of the International Social Security Association	56-15865	#1771735
6.	Labor relations reference manual	39-10217	#1755409
7.	The Source book of American state legislation	82-642083	#6181988
8.	Case and comment	sn82-7976	#8789037
9.	Euskal urtekari estatistikoa	84-640037	#10260281
10.	California. Dept. of Water Resources. Transactions under the Davis-Grunsky Act	sc84-7050	#1552399

D. Proceedings information

1.	Current trends in life sciences	sf83-2017	#7087481
2.	Advances in biomaterials	sf83-2004	#6832932
3.	Tropical diseases research series	sf83-2013	#6168790
4.	Advances in myocardiology	80-643989	#6353133
5.	Washington State Entomological Society. Proceedings of the Washington State Entomological Society	82-646578	#1663476
6.	Advances in data base theory	sn82-20071	#7399682
7.	Developments in food carbohydrate	83-640905	#4532240

8. Conference on Application of   82-642132   #1461274
   X-ray Analysis. Advances
   in x-ray analysis.
9.
10. Fracture mechanics of   83-641076   #4298543
    ceramics
11. Clinical science. Supplement   sn80-2765   #6297497
12. Advanced geriatric medicine   sc82-7382   #8230324
13. Australian mining and   82-643157   #7065636
    petroleum law journal
14. Publications of the Texas Folk-   16-6413   #1767350
    lore Society
15. American journal of physiology   a43-3158   #1480180
16. The Clinical biochemist.   sc83-1303   #8944059
    Reviews

E. General coverage information
1. Labor market information for   83-640504   #7066166
   affirmative action pro-
   grams (Virginia Employment Commission. Man-
   power Research Division).
   Supplement
2. Serie encuestas. Opinión   82-645023   #8712564
   empresarial del sector
   industrial
3. Estadísticas de comercio   78-646435   #4009661
   exterior
4. Curriculum development   sn83-10187   #6677031
   library. Cumulative index.
5. Ingreso y producto, Puerto   77-640669   #3278795
   Rico
6. Costs of producing livestock in   82-642804   #8363496
   the United States
7. Iowa. Dept. of Transportation.   82-646782   #7438797
   Planning and research
   program
8. National Research Council   82-647078   #8605610
   (U.S.). Issues and studies
9. Magill's cinema annual   83-644357   #9315435
10. South Pacific bibliography   84-641270   #9921005
11. Art book review   sc83-1010   #8758334
12. Shichōson ni okeru chiiki   83-642823   #9439803
    seisaku no dōkō no
    gaiyō

13.	Aeronautical Research Council (Great Britain). Reports and memoranda	48-30623	#1751414
14.	Oregon. Dept. of Education. Career and Vocational Education Section. Planning for vocational education in Oregon	82-642268	#8957504
15.	Residents in Wisconsin adult correctional institutions and community correctional residential centers on . . . with five-year trends for . . .	79-643433	#5229615
16.	Direction of trade statistics. Yearbook	82-646788	#7866916
17.	Indice de ciências sociais	sn82-20585	#5973286
18.	Guide to U.S. government maps: geologic and hydrologic maps	sn83-10278	#4660069
19.	British Library. Lending Division. British reports, translations and theses	81-643525	#7432736

F. General translation notes

1.	Khimiĭa i tekhnologiĭa vody	83-644945	#8558750
2.	Soviet sports review	82-647330	#5214378
3.	Rheinisch-Westfälisches Elektrizitätswerk Aktiengesellschaft. Annual report for the fiscal year	sc83-5188	#9348185
4.	Soviet scientific reviews. Section D. Biology reviews	83-642277	#6998955
5.	Chinese sociology and anthropology	77-4280	#1548629
6.	Chinese physics	81-643627	#7052624
7.	Mapping sciences and remote sensing	sn84-7112	#11120779
8.	Brazilian economic studies	76-645439	#2515839
9.	Abstracts in German anthropology	sn82-20587	#7562980
10.	The Journal of the Acoustical Society of Japan (E)	sn82-20579	#7057795
11.	Bibliography of modern Hebrew literature in translation	81-644248	#6038553

II. NOTES ABOUT TITLES

A. Title proper information
1. Wisconsin. Emergency Number 82-644709 #8673093
Systems Board. Annual
report on the operations
of the 911 Emergency
Numbers Systems Board
in Wisconsin
2. Entertainment law journal sc82-6830 #8141124
(Entertainment Law Jour-
nal Association)
3. District of Columbia. Acts 80-641003 #5965065
affecting the District of
Columbia
4. Katei zasshi 83-645830 #9921382
5. Open letter cn76-300161 #2096108
6. Analisis geoeconomico ... sc83-2199 #9348577
7. Compensation (Washington, 82-645698 #8370349
D.C. : 1982)
8. Faglige bidrag 75-644078 #4354330
9. Hompō keizai tōkei 28-30743 #2239062
10. Bulletin (Holmes Safety 82-643960 #5140851
Association)
11. A Census of HMOs sc82-3169 #3291674
12. Oral History Association. sc80-1274 #5266585
Membership directory
13. A Journal of female liberation sc80-826 #1754586
14. Chilton's I & C S 83-646306 #9673774

B. Other title information
1. Försäkringstidningen 61-45524 #9462767
(Stockholm, Sweden)
2. National woodlands sn81-1143 #7085730
3. Case and comment sn82-7976 #8789037
4. Öl und Kohle sn83-5728 #9659417
5. Fortschritte auf dem Gebiete sf84-1046 #1644093
der Röntgenstrahlen und
der Nuklearmedizin.
Ergänzungsband
6. Essays in contemporary 82-642433 #7850402
economic problems
7. Advance data from vital & 79-643688 #2778178
health statistics of the
National Center for Health
Statistics

8.	Distilled Spirits Council of the U.S. DISCUS facts book	77-641483	#3624938
9.	Studies in formative spirituality	84-641552	#5156328
10.	Aspen journal for the arts	sn82-455	#8262129
11.	Indian Academy of Sciences. Proceedings of the Indian Academy of Sciences. Section A	36-11636	#2673275

C. Language of title/parallel title information

1.	Lingvaj problemoj kaj lingvo-planado	sn80-8496	#3805689
2.	Education. Whites	82-643935	#8560925
3.	Community health in SA	sc84-1095	#10106139
4.	Belgium. Parlement. Parlementaire docu-mentatie	83-640944	#9189536
5.	Education. Whites	82-643935	#8560925
6.	Études de statistique agricole		#2927584
7.	Groundwater series (Pretoria)	sf83-9020	#2361386
8.	Regionalstatistik årbog	sn83-10936	#8291363
9.	Annales entomologici fennici		#6134600
10.	South African Library Associa-tion. Jaarverslag	sc82-2493	#8801326
11.	Filatelist	82-646932	#9014917
12.	Technical report (Skipjack Survey and Assessment Programme)	sn83-10411	#8541060
13.	Ingreso y producto, Puerto Rico	77-640669	#3278795
14.	Nepāla (Kathmandu, Nepal)	82-647210	#9059433
15.	Bibliografía ecuatoriana	77-649113	#4432658
16.	Electric power in Canada	73-645063	#1787807
17.	Igaku sensui	sc83-2764	#8803090

D. Names of titles within a serial (not issued separately)

1.	Baldwin's Ohio tax service	83-640560	#6480527
2.	Chartered Institute of Trans-port. Journal	sn82-20904	#3050714
3.	Health, United States	76-641496	#3151554
4.	Applied radiology	80-643438	#3783853

5.	Dr. A. Petermann's Mitteilungen aus Justus Perthes' geographischer Anstalt	sf83-6896	#5860725
6.			
7.	Coin & medal news	83-641852	#8302946
8.	The Nautical almanac for the year ...	sc79-2685	#1286390
9.	Serials in the British Library (Annual)	sn84-10171	#8264921
10.	Dawes family newsletter	83-640408	#9157629
11.	Garden supply retailer	82-645629	#5303894
12.	Aqua-field sportsman	84-641431	#10446729
13.	Academy of Accounting Historians. Membership roster		#6865903

E.   Varying forms of title

1.	United States. Office of Management and Budget. Budget of the United States government	70-611049	#932137
2.	Food and Agriculture Organization of the United Nations. Statistics Division. An Annual review of world production, consumption, and trade of fertilizers	55-739	#2916025
3.	Rêde Ferroviária Federal, S.A. Relatório anual	83-641830	#5141169
4.	Oil & petrochemical pollution	84-642414	#9250569
5.	Chilton's distribution worldwide (1977)	sc83-7071	#589834
6.	The South Central bulletin	83-642124	#2740893
7.	Current trends in life sciences	sf83-2017	#7087481
8.	Ethnic racial brotherhood	80-641850	#6525120
9.	Bibliografía ecuatoriana	77-649113	#4432658
10.	Golden Gate University. School of Law. Golden Gate University law review	sn82-7120	#9034010
11.	Knitting times	74-645022	#1794210
12.	Mississippi game and fish	sn78-744	#1758363
13.	Zambia. Central Statistical Office. National accounts ... and input-output table	82-640310	#5753666

14.	Acta mathematica Universitatis Comenianae	sn83-10124	#8412045
15.	Haiku Bungakukan kujō	83-641935	#9310213
16.	State government research checklist	sn79-4788	#4736514

F. Alternate issues

1.	Institute of Management Sciences. TIMS/ORSA bulletin	76-643088	#2471224
2.	Suid-Afrikaanse tydskrif vir biblioteeken inligtingwese	82-642415	#7980432
3.	Abstracts of Bulgarian scientific literature. Geosciences	81-641638	#6799592
4.	Occupational employment trends in the State of Oregon	82-642603	#7630449
5.	ASHRAE handbook		#8009578
6.	Early child development and care: ECDC	82-640509	#1772625
7.	Modern brewery age	sn81-5449	#6392377

III. IMPRINT VARIATION INFORMATION

1.	Camera lucida	83-646300	#6430212
2.	Letras femeninas	81-642380	#3816008
3.	Advances in cladistics	83-646412	#9820449
4.	Boston Society of Landscape Architects. Annual report	sc82-4345	#8412345
5.	International Congress on High Speed Photography and Photonics. Proceedings of the International Congress on High Speed Photography and Photonics	sn83-10800	#5671260
6.	Beiträge zur Volkskunde der Ungardeutschen	sc83-8037	#9104157
7.	Alcheringa (New York, N.Y.)	72-626511	#1780749
8.	Decorative art and modern interiors	sc83-3099	#1781874
9.	Congress on Research in Dance. CORD newsletter	sc82-2282	#8530503

IV. ISSUING INFORMATION

A. Format

1.	Biblioinformación cafetera	sn82-22195	#4738783
2.	Peasant studies newsletter	sn83-10622	#1963832
3.	Encyclopédie permanente, Japon	82-640488	#6344244
4.	National sales tax rate directory	82-646612	#8342190
5.	America buys : Updating service	sn82-22060	#7570064
6.	Employee benefits cases	81-642948	#7033880
7.	Oregon Land Use Board of Appeals decisions	80-70149	#7064196
8.	NAHB builder	80-647970	#6192906
9.	Collected original resources in education		#3250843
10.	Flue	sc82-4472	#8150495
11.	Financial Accounting Standards Board. FASB discussion memorandum		#1864609
12.	Bibliographic guide to law	79-642569	#2282334
13.	Library of Congress. Subject Cataloging Division. Subject headings in microform	79-641066	#3454199

B. Updates and revisions

1.	Burrelle's New Jersey media directory	sn83-10630	#7119047
2.	International mail manual	sn83-10632	#8269582
3.	Maps on file	sn81-791	#7240499
4.	United States. Patent and Trademark Office. Office of Documentation, Planning, Support, and Control. Manual of classification		#4859604
5.	Directory of government officials ... federal, state, county, city, township and special district officials in North Dakota	83-640446	#8938143
6.	Pay scales in the California state civil service	46-27570	#8880233
7.	Uniform crime reports for the United States	30-27005	#2165904

8.	A Bibliography of ab initio molecular wave functions. Supplement for . . .	82-646873	#8301811
9.	Eurostatistik	80-648763	#5144628
10.	United States. Legislation on foreign relations through . . .	83-640253	#3700343
11.	Automotive literature index	82-643376	#7289023
12.	Labor-management relations in the public service	81-645131	#5191433
13.	A List of references: maize virus diseases and corn stunt	sn82-22220	#7541620
14.	Bureau of National Affairs (Washington, D.C.). Environmental reporter. Federal laws		#3373471
15.	Multiple input productivity indexes	sn83-11454	#7941334

C.   Miscellaneous issuing information

1.	Mukashi	83-646483	#10028803
2.	Indiana Stream Pollution Control Board. State of Indiana water pollution control program plan	83-645852	#6934812
3.	UNDEX. United Nations documents index. Series A: subject index	79-13748	#1107959
4.	Electronic publishing abstracts	84-642000	#9960391
5.	Annual survey of family law	83-641536	#7702984
6.	The Annual of the British school at Athens	19-19615	#1537363
7.	American Helicopter Society. Annual forum proceedings	sn82-21296	#7315648
8.	Trenie i iznos. English	83-642867	#7810251
9.	Direction of trade statistics	81-649851	#7154584
10.	Transportation safety information report	81-641374	#5166195
11.	Building services & environmental engineer	sn82-22261	#5249236
12.	Godishnik na Visshiĭa institut po arkhitektura i stroitelstvo, Sofiĭa	82-647154	#8162066
13.	Disabled USA	77-643096	#3322866
14.	NOAA technical report NMFS SSRF	83-644784	#1522427

15. Transportation safety informa-   81-641374   #5166195
    tion report
16. California. Dept. of Water   #1213170
    Resources.   Bulletin
17. North American applied animal   sn82-22223   #8523487
    ethology newsletter

V.   MISCELLANEOUS GENERAL NOTES

1. Advances in fertility research   sn82-2610   #8393092
2. 50,000 leading U.S.   sn81-6206   #6352772
   corporations
3. Climatological data. National   79-643781   #4447360
   summary
4. Abbay   80-646507   #6825901
5. Frauenberuf   sc83-1064   #7338884
6. Journal of studies on alcohol   sc83-7250   #5916226
7. Council of Europe. Committee   83-641236   #9201437
   of Ministers.   Resolutions
8. North Dakota rules of court,   82-646714   #8543155
   with amendments received
   to ...
9. Annual statistical report of the 82-647305   #5576999
   Superintendent of Public
   Instruction
10. Annales de physique   49-52171   #1481283
11. Cuadernos panamericanos de   sn83-10763   #8247530
    información geográfica
12. Suid-Afrika se kommersiële   82-646953   #7603824
    houtbronne
13. Current developments in copy-   82-642095   #4279222
    right law
14. Missouri. Land Reclamation   82-644645   #8238272
    Commission. Abandoned
    Mine Land Section.
    Annual report of the Aban-
    doned Mine Land Section
15. Science, technology, and   81-640299   #6742417
    American diplomacy
    (Washington, D.C. : 1980)
16. Le Guide arabe pour le   53-32838   #3819945
    commerce, l'industrie &
    les professions libérales
    dans les pays arabes
17. Annual report of the Coxcatlan   82-646660   #4610575
    Project

18.	Handbook for employees transferring to Spain	sn83-10354	#7261042
19.	Farmer cooperatives	76-646745	#2200788
20.	United Nations. Economic Commission for Europe. Annual bulletin of housing and building statistics for Europe	60-2123	#1261977
21.	Demographic yearbook	50-641	#1168223
22.	Current industrial reports. MQ-22Q. Carpet and rugs	82-645446	#2547072
23.	Book report (Columbus, Ohio)	82-645647	#8187197
24.	Designers West	81-641142	#4087182
25.	Journal of geophysical research	83-641459	#3918314
26.	Hoy	78-646252	#4181058
27.	Complete desk reference of veterinary pharmaceuticals & geologicals (Media, Pa.)	sn82-20903	#5933707
28.	National Academy of Sciences (U.S.). Proceedings of the National Academy of Sciences of the United States of America	16-10069	#1607201
29.	California yearbook (California Almanac Company)	82-645580	#4758346
30.	Progress in the prevention and control of air pollution in . . .	82-646574	#2902992

515 NUMBERING PECULIARITIES NOTE

I. REPORT YEAR COVERAGE

1. Botswana. Ministry of Finance and Development Planning. National development plan   82-642148   #8401470
2. Current industrial reports. MQ-C1, Survey of plant capacity   81-649750   #3811904
3. Gumma Kenritsu Rekishi Hakubutsukan. Gumma Kenritsu Rekishi Hakubutsukan nempo   82-643434   #8482883
4. Statistics Canada. Education, Science and Culture Division. Financial Information Section. Federal and provincial student aid in Canada   74-641908   #1792315
5. Istituto universitario navale (Naples, Italy)   82-640015   #7602647
6. Quarterly executive trend report   83-642538   #9397009
7. A Financial analysis of the for-hire tank truck industry for the year . . .   sc83-1049   #3808610
8. U.S.-Japan Cooperative Cancer Research Program. Progress report   83-640506   #4750211
9. Société anonyme Cockerill-Ougrée. Report and accounts presented at the general meeting of shareholders   sc83-4030   #9032637
10. Illinois. Office of the State Treasurer. Treasurer's semi-annual report   83-640271   #9135474
11. Citrus fruits by states . . .   82-642464   #8320201
12. National Foundation for Infantile Paralysis. Annual report   sf82-8043   #1605984

13.	Equalized assessed valuations and tax rates	sn83-10251	#8163438
14.	Monthly Florida motor gasoline consumption	84-640160	#10344654
15.	Statistics, Public School Finance Division	79-643332	#5121099
16.	Report of funds granted to Delaware during fiscal year . . . by State agency and by Federal program (OMB number)	82-646944	#9021855
17.	Ireland. National Board for Science and Technology. Annual report for the year ended 31 Dec. . . .	82-644179	#8602620
18.	Montréal (Québec). Annual report	82-644940	#6679961
19.	Maryland. Criminal Justice Information Advisory Board. Annual report to the Governor and the General Assembly	82-646410	#8925147
20.	Federal offenders in the United States district courts	81-644313	#1681076
21.	Connecticut. Office of Policy & Management. Statewide facility and capital plan	81-646396	#7636440
22.	United States. Environmental Data Service. International decade of ocean exploration	78-644884	#2679186

II.   DOUBLE NUMBERING

1.			
2.	Videha	73-904759	#8014499
3.	Domestic engineering and the journal of mechanical contracting	sf84-1000	#1781876
4.	Mexico. President. State of the nation report to the Mexican Congress	83-645133	#8267448

5.	L'Information grammaticale	sc82-4499	#8919780
6.	Arkansas. State Board for Vocational Education. Arkansas annual plan for vocational education, PL94-482	83-640850	#5516335
7.	East and west (Rome, Italy)	56-33103	#1567218
8.	Analele Universităţii Bucureşti. Acta logica	sc83-3075	#3507383
9.	The Bellingham review	82-644979	#3689085
10.	Il Nuovo cimento della Società italiana di fisica. D, Condensed matter, atomic, molecular and chemical physics, biophysics	sc82-3630	#8724239
11.	Alabama medicaid	82-646241	#9035826
12.	Acta oecologica. OEcologia plantarum	81-645733	#6257682
13.	Classical antiquity	83-640320	#7870789
14.	Isotope geoscience		#9428986
15.	American Council on Education studies. Series VI, Student personnel work	39-15476	#3511884
16.	Commentationes physico-mathematicae. Dissertationes	sf83-2055	#8191871
17.	Gazeta Rabochego i krest'ianskogo pravitel'stva	sc82-7594	#7032981
18.	Journal of the Chemical Society. Faraday transactions 1	sn79-4663	#1034405
19.	American Philosophical Society. Proceedings of the American Philosophical Society	sn78-683	#9292549
20.	UFSI reports	sn81-2316	#7939882
21.	United States. National Commission for Employment Policy. Annual report to the President and the Congress of the National Commission for Employment Policy	80-648291	#6564180
22.	Allergy supplementum	sc83-2189	#9232400
23.	The New York Jewish week	83-642782	#9144716
24.	al-Wa'y al-Islāmī	ne68-4659	#2178455

III. COMBINED ISSUES OR VOLUMES

1.	Current industrial reports. Mattresses, foundations and sleep furniture	81-649769	#3081040
2.	New World Archaeological Foundation. Papers of the New World Archaeo- logical Foundation	60-41468	#1142787
3.	Art and poetry today	78-914394	#5817473
4.	Acta mathematica Academiae Scientiarum Hungaricae	54-20368	#1460914
5.	European file	sf81-7023	#5211930
6.	Community mental health review	79-643403	#2381437
7.	Artpark	82-642102	#3819051
8.	The Florida genealogist	82-646389	#3957742
9.	Afro American journal of philosophy	84-644990	#10149260
10.	Indiana University. President. The President's report	52-62053	#8717702
11.	Chemical dependencies	81-640950	#7111945
12.	Svobodnoe slovo (Mount Vernon, N.Y.)	82-644421	#8412883
13.	Anuario energia eléctrica	sn84-10164	#10121473
14.	Ethnic racial brotherhood	80-641850	#6525120

IV. NUMBERING INCONSISTENCIES OR IRREGULARITIES

A. Numbering lacking

1.	Hans David Billman family bulletin	83-642404	#9372683
2.	Bulletin du Centre d'études et de recherche scientifiques	62-58596	#9347914
3.	Najmat al-Baḥrayn	83-646709	#10054076
4.	Desertification control	82-643809	#8543455
5.	The Numbers news	sc82-4133	#7757812
6.	73 amateur radio	sn82-20020	#4364872
7.	Japanese religions	83-645874	#6548536
8.	Geosur	82-643195	#8427052
9.	Market Technicians Associa- tion journal	82-645234	#8744678
10.	Flue	sc82-4472	#8150495
11.	50,000 leading U.S. corporations	sn81-6206	#6352772

12.	Bibliografía latinoamericana. 1, Trabajos publicados por latinoamericanos en revistas extranjeras	84-640870	#10353036
13.	Bulletin (Geological Survey of British Guiana)	sf82-8049	#1287373
14.	Beiträge zur Gerontologie und Altenarbeit	sn84-5166	#9870807
15.	Early modern Europe today	sn83-10751	#8774049
16.	Materialy po geticheskoĭ i eksperimental'noĭ mineralogii	66-49173	#2617230
17.	Evaluation	73-640899	#1784879
18.	Itinerario	sn83-10746	#5624669
19.	New road . . .	a43-3687	#2409801
20.	The Virginia economic review	84-642766	#1550102

B. Numbering dropped

1.	Design engineering (London, England)	82-640070	#6237037
2.	U.S.-Japan Cooperative Cancer Research Program. Progress report	83-640506	#4750211
3.	National woodlands	sn81-1143	#7085730
4.	Journal of economic studies (Bradford, West Yorkshire)	82-645768	#1001112
5.	Disabled USA	77-643096	#3322866
6.	The Communist	81-649127	#4675593
7.	Disabled USA	77-643096	#3322866
8.	Skyscraper management	ca33-801	#1765613

C. Numbering added

1.	Monthly Detroit	83-640481	#3524336
2.	EDIS : Environmental Data and Information Service	79-640361	#4359560
3.	The Pierre-Fort Pierre Genealogical Society	83-642845	#9445548
4.	Research proceedings (University of Delhi. Dept. of Anthropology)	82-913340	#3863839
5.	International railway journal and rapid transit review : IRJ	81-641150	#6070542
6.	Review of books and religion (Forward Movement Publications)	82-642834	#7961056

7.	Metropolitan Life Insurance Company. Statistical bulletin	31-30794	#1757228

D. Numbering errors

1.	Transactions of the Indiana State Medical Society	sc82-1366	#7065529
2.	Arts & architecture	46-32251	#1514368
3.	Critical mass energy journal	sn81-4626	#7136089
4.	Le Praticien. Supplément au no . . .	sc82-4474	#8852991
5.	Garden supply retailer	82-645629	#5303894
6.	Family therapy	73-640444	#1731055
7.	Modern brewery age	sn81-5449	#6392377
8.	The Field artilleryman	83-642607	#9399559
9.	Illinois. Dept. of Mines and Minerals. Coal report of Illinois	sc80-1080	#2371496
10.	National Association of Retail Druggists. NARD journal	80-644613	#1695474
11.	The Progressive	33-15217	#1762985
12.	The Candle of Phi Upsilon Omicron		#5130878
13.	Ebony	52-42074	#1567306
14.	Education directory, colleges & universities	83-645625	#2575450
15.	Analele Universităţii Bucureşti. Seria acta logica	66-47376	#8909820
16.	Abrasive Engineering Society (U.S.). Conference/ Exhibition. Proceedings.	82-645670	#6296946
17.	The Ampleforth review	sc82-4469	#5539960
18.	National Association of Retail Druggists. NARD newsletter	78-645112	#4102933
19.	Employment hours and earnings, Virginia	82-645932	#7766075
20.	Municipal review & AMA news	82-647392	#7386722
21.	Urban planning reports	sc82-1368	#6829048
22.	The NAHB news	83-641518	#7912857
23.	Wen i (Hong Kong)	82-647228	#7839743
24.	Journal of the Inter-American Foundation	82-646994	#4862949
25.	Indiana. Laws of the State of Indiana, passed at the . . . session of the General Assembly	7-31549	#8733001

26. Association of College   #2292888
    Unions -International.
    Proceedings of the annual
    conference of the Associa-
    tion of College Unions -
    International

E. Numbering shared with other titles
    1. Brief   #1537076
    2. Domestic cars mechanical   81-643746   #7434866
       parts/labor estimating
       guide
    3. Society of Petroleum Engineers sn82-6229   #2461356
       of AIME. Transactions of
       the Society of Petroleum
       Engineers of the American
       Institute of Mining,
       Metallurgical, and
       Petroleum Engineers, Inc.
    4. Biomedicine express   sc80-2047   #1636173
    5. Ferroelectrics Letters section sn82-935   #8209340
    6. American studies international   76-649667   #2077111
    7. Acta pathological et   sc83-3060   #7339040
       microbiologica
       Scandinavica. Supplement
    8. Indian journal of physics and   sa68-11993   #3639756
       proceedings of the Indian
       Association for the
       Cultivation of Science
    9. Mutation research. Mutation   sn81-3918   #7356055
       research letters

F. Numbering that does not begin with
       vol. 1
    1. Québec (Province). Régie du   84-641958   #10521046
       logement.   Décisions de
       la Régie du logement
    2. Urban outlook   sc82-1294   #8445335
    3. Ukrainian mathematical journal sf78-501   #1496592
    4. Today's education.   81-643036   #6840763
       Mathematics/science
       edition
    5. Le Praticien. Supplément au   sc82-4474   #8852991
       no . . .

6.	Great Britain. Parliament. House of Commons. Parliamentary debates (Hansard)	10-3568	#8985610
7.	Adansonia	sf82-4090	#1461074
8.	Journal of experimental psychology: Human learning and memory	76-643081	#1172614
9.	International yearbook of education	49-48323	#1753766
10.	Journal de physique. Lettres	sn81-4452	#1318711
11.	Deutsche optische Wochen-schrift und Central-Zeitung für Optik und Mechanik (Docentra)	sf83-1012	#8828735
12.	Bollettino della Unione matematica italiana. Sez. C: Analisi funzionale e applicazioni	sn83-10601	#7880785
13.	American archives of rehabili-tation therapy	sn80-1695	#1479313
14.	Boletín de Instituto Español de Oceanografía (1977)	82-645020	#8714537
15.	Colección estudios CIEPLAN	82-646207	#6175141

G. Inconsistencies in chronological designations

1.	Sound heritage series	sn82-20153	#7136846
2.	Branka	82-646905	#9013181
3.	Common stock indexes	sc82-4481	#8417735
4.	The Arup journal	sc83-7004	#8838510
5.	Art west	83-643043	#4543340
6.	Douglas County Illinois Genealogical Society : [newsletter]	83-647615	#10176466
7.	Estatística básica de arrecadação	83-642491	#6765943
8.	The Field artilleryman	83-642607	#9399559
9.	American Association of Exporters and Importers. Membership directory	sn84-10436	#8329516
10.	Les Annales de la recherche urbaine	sn82-22055	#5856529
11.	Directory of employee organizations in New York State	76-620003	#5093230

12.	Bridge (Belgrade, Serbia)	66-9922	#2652059
13.	The Register of the American Saddlebred Horse Association (incorporated)	82-647022	#8264831

H. Miscellaneous numbering inconsistencies or irregularities

1.	The JAG journal	52-66952	#1449089
2.	Design book review : DBR	83-646132	#9361004
3.	Calendar (California Debt Advisory Commission)	sc84-8099	#10068625
4.	Boletim mensal (Banco de Fomento Nacional)	82-647030	#9033750
5.	Sexually transmitted diseases. Abstracts & bibliography	79-644375	#5093205
6.	Soviet Union	51-36672	#1642588
7.	Soviet soil science	61-675	#1587583
8.	Commission of the European Communities. Directorate-General for Agriculture. Newsletter on the common agricultural policy		#5794632
9.	Directory information service	77-641771	#3208182
10.	al-Muntadá	83-646285	#9999436
11.	Collier bankruptcy cases	75-643843	#2241453
12.	The Economic bulletin of Ghana	67-122046	#8186026
13.	Publications of the American Statistical Association		#1680935
14.	Jen min wen hsüeh	83-648239	#1605226
15.	New guard bulletin	83-645987	#4811308
16.	Sverkhtverdye materialy	84-642684	#9820773
17.	Rand Corporation. A Rand note	sn83-10953	#1583244
18.	Journal of geophysical research. Space physics	83-641459	#3918314
19.	Official airline guide (North American edition)	sc83-9407	#1077891
20.	Book review digest	6-24490	#6038062
21.	Modern brewery age	sn81-5449	#6392377
22.	Classical rag (Silver Spring, Md.)	83-640269	#9135086
23.	Joint Computer Conference. Proceedings of the . . . Joint Computer Conference	sc79-2521	#4683874
24.	Ancestors west	82-645233	#8744728

V. ISSUING PECULIARITIES

A. General issuing peculiarities

1.	Comparative studies, cross-national summaries	82-643523	#7869905
2.	Keynote (New York, N.Y. : 1983)	sc83-7085	#2448119
3.	California. Dept. of Water Resources. Bulletin		#1213170
4.	Pubblicazioni dell'Osservatorio "G. Horn d'Arturo"	sc82-3652	#8905607
5.	Montana. Legislature. Senate and House journals of the . . . Legislature of the State of Montana commencing in special session . . . and ending . . .	82-645227	#8744637
6.	ICP software directory (1981)	82-647332	#8074041
7.	Gaceta del gobierno de Guatemala	83-644068	#9655855
8.	Bulletin signalétique. 225, Tectonique, géophysique interne	83-641972	#8327316
9.	The Eastern economist	49-20208	#1567281
10.	Occupational health & safety (Waco, Tex.)	82-641424	#2214952
11.	United States. Bureau of Radiological Health. Office of the Associate Director for Administration. Technical Information Staff. Bureau of Radiological Health publications index	79-642649	#4430580
12.	Academy of Accounting Historians. Working paper series	sn83-10057	#4874242
13.	Ch'ŏngsaekchi	83-641378	#9228280
14.	Annex 21	sn82-22044	#8568502
15.	Newsletter (Scientists' Center for Animal Welfare (Washington, D.C.))	sc83-8343	#4656277
16.	Indian Academy of Sciences. Proceedings of the Indian Academy of Sciences	36-11636	#2673275

17.	JGR, Journal of geophysical research	80-643369	
18.	Meridians	82-641387	#7906012
19.	Advances in psychology (Amsterdam, Netherlands)	sf83-1005	#5253350
20.	Arnoldia, Zimbabwe Rhodesia		#8223338
21.	Industrial Relations Research Association. Membership directory of the Industrial Relations Research Association	sn82-20931	#5812981
22.	Summary of legislative action on the budget bill	sc82-3533	#8732677
23.	Progress toward regulatory reform	sc83-1312	#9086578
24.	Annales d'immunologie	sn80-13574	#1643402
25.	Acta pathologica, microbiologica, et immunologica Scandinavica. Supplement	sc83-3061	#8661455
26.	Analytical letters	sn80-45	#1481079
27.	Management science	sc83-7084	#4827722
28.	The Biochemical journal	26-11128	#1532962
29.	Washington University (Saint Louis, Mo.). Washington University studies	18-8774	#1644739
30.	USSR report. Life sciences. Effect of nonionizing electromagnetic radiation (Public ed.)	sc83-3009	#8525784
31.	Progress in planning	83-640193	#1049759
32.	Bibliographic index of health education periodi- cals : BIHEP	82-646381	#7754004

B. Number of issues per volume, etc.

1.	The Journal for special educators	80-644999	#4409595
2.	Biochemistry international	81-649182	#674187
3.	Chemical geology	77-3539	#1553973
4.	Monographs on music, dance, and theatre in Asia	83-640375	#9150653
5.	Environmental pollution. Series A, Ecological and biological	81-643637	#6067650

	6.	Urban affairs papers	83-644053	#6460674
	7.	Social security bulletin. Annual statistical supplement	sc77-385	#1939422
	8.	Current industrial reports. Mattresses, foundations and sleep furniture	81-649769	#3081040
	9.	Tōyō Bunko (Japan). Tōyō Bunko nenpō	sc82-3673	#8921273
	10.	Career education quarterly	81-641275	#4571463
C.		Issued in named parts, sections, etc.		
	1.	The annual of advertising & editorial art & design of the Art Directors Club of New York		#3939655
	2.	National Library of Medicine (U.S.). Index-catalogue of the Library of the Surgeon General's Office, National Library of Medicine	sc82-3693	#8624010
	3.	Bureau of Medical Devices standards survey (United States. Bureau of Medical Devices)	81-640909	#4315895
	4.	California state rail plan	sc82-6153	#8922519
	5.	Global banking directory	82-646200	#8913588
	6.	American history	82-643952	#8231094
	7.	Local area personal income	80-641946	#3622072
	8.	National accounts (Organisation for Economic Co-operation and Development. Dept. of Economics and Statistics)	sc84-8563	#9420508
	9.			
	10.	The . . . Study of media and markets	sc82-7498	#7233459
	11.	Handbook of Latin American studies	36-32633	#1751732
	12.	Encyclopedia of associations	76-46129	#1223579
D.		Issued in unnamed parts, sections, etc.		
	1.	Associations' publications in print	81-17005	#8008221
	2.	Ethnic information sources of the United States	84-640146	#9536958

3.	Online database search services directory	84-642259	#10062770
4.			
5.	Directory of American scholars	57-9125	#1246775
6.	Industriens struktur og aktiviteter	83-645632	#7058185
7.	GeoSciTech citation index	83-642674	#8297273
8.	Annual communications law institute	82-641723	#8166137
9.	American Institute of Architects. AIA journal	46-21775	#4368512
10.	Geological Society of America. Geological Society of America bulletin	1-23380	#1570691
11.	Allgemeine deutsche Bibliothek	7-23735	#1479144
12.	Arctic Institute of North America. Library. Catalogue. Supplement	75-646581	#4265207
13.	Avery Library. Catalog of the Avery Memorial Architectural Library of Columbia University. Second edition, enlarged. Supplement	75-649442	#2244927
14.	North central North Dakota genealogical record	83-640311	#8147331
15.	Hoppea	83-640249	#9129932
16.	Bell & Howell Co. Indexing Center. Bell & Howell's newspaper index to the Washington post	80-640592	#5972290
17.	Situación de la oferta de vivienda en España en . . .	82-641815	#8275919
18.	American Institute for Decision Sciences. Meeting. Proceedings	82-646173	#1667466
19.	al-Arshīf al-ṣuḥufī	82-645613	#8815992
20.	Register for earned income taxes	82-647165	#9055107
21.	Catalogue des thèses et écrits académiques	83-642231	#6445170

E. Multiple or revised editions
    1. The Poetical register, and repository of fugitive poetry for . . .   12-22988   #2266289
    2. American Society for Testing and Materials. Annual book of ASTM standards. Pt. 42, Emission, molecular, and mass spectroscopy, chromatography, resinography, microscopy, computerized systems, surface analysis   83-641658   #2187052
    3. Control engineering   sc83-4127   #6592268
    4. Agriculture handbook (United States. Dept. of Agriculture)   73-644869   #1573294
    5. Basic (Pell) grant validation handbook   81-642713   #7616530
    6. Chronicle vocational school manual   82-643014   #7320922
    7. Bradway-Broadway bulletin   84-640285   #10263479
    8. Colorado air quality data report   82-646887   #8877767
    9. United States. Dept. of Energy. Congressional budget request   80-643192   #4837750
    10. Directory of Soviet officials   84-640183   #2197616
    11. Imported collision estimating guide   81-642225   #7546402

F. Cumulations
    1. Employment and earnings, United States   80-644780   #958410
    2. Federal software exchange catalog   83-643654   #3454211
    3. Advance annotation service to the Code of Virginia   sc83-9199   #7921297
    4. Bell & Howell newspaper index to the New Orleans times-picayune, the States-item   sn81-148   #7054855
    5. Federal immigration law reporter   84-640150   #9293065
    6. Computer program abstracts   76-604507   #1564604
    7. Index of federal specifications, standards and commercial item descriptions   80-643534   #5730039

8.	Food bibliography	83-644044	#6688720
9.	Catalogue of British official publications not published by HMSO	sn82-20910	#7678038
10.	The Forum index	83-648059	#9674340
11.	Cartel (Austin, Tex.)	84-642461	#2256041
12.	The Foundation Center source book profiles	77-79015	#3718433
13.	Text-Index : TI	sc83-5028	#7789814
14.	Statistical reference index . . . annual	81-645886	#7568304

VI.   PRELIMINARY ISSUES

1.	Contemporary orthopaedics	sc83-1114	#5057206
2.	South (London, England)	84-645374	#7309028
3.	EC trade with the ACP states and the south Mediterranean states	82-647311	#5968193
4.	Africus	82-643661	#8514634
5.	Garden design	82-647188	#8610163
6.	Newsletter on education and training programmes for specialized information personnel	sn82-20047	#5533585
7.			
8.	Computer business news	sc83-8104	#4181247
9.	Automation news (New York, N.Y.)	sc83-8566	#9114303
10.	The McKinney maze	82-647333	#9078483
11.	Quality progress	sc83-8122	#6569242
12.	Assessors journal	70-3958	#1514495
13.	Doctoral dissertations in history	77-640363	#2429011
14.	Art digest/South newsletter	sn82-20227	#3855229
15.	America, history and life	64-25630	#1479243

VII.   SUSPENSION OF PUBLICATION

1.			
2.	El Iniciador	a43-3100	#1586905
3.	The Dance journal	82-643577	#4877180
4.	Maritime	73-11160	#1756696
5.	Trade union information	57-24345	#6201585
6.	Writings on American history	4-8590	#1770230

VIII. ITEMS NOT PUBLISHED

1.	EAR	sc82-3313	#6887600
2.	Evaluation and change	sc82-8179	#6504146
3.	AV guide	sc83-1140	#3867076
4.	FAO commodity review and outlook	a63-278	#2720294
5.	Annales de géographie	sn79-9782	#3341949
6.	Cleveland Electrical/ Electronics. Conference and Exposition. CECON . . . record	84-643223	#5098134
7.	Conference on Application of X-ray Analysis. Advances in x-ray analysis	82-642132	#1461274
8.	Association of Collegiate Schools of Architecture. Proceedings of the ACSA annual meeting	80-643592	#5384757
9.	Accademia nazionale dei Lincei. Annuario della Accademia nazionale dei Lincei	52-28690	#6340475
10.	Journal of American insurance	sc83-5089	#5692000
11.	Bibliography of agriculture with subject index	63-24851	#2743878
12.	Beadle's popular library		#8357938
13.	Bulletin signalétique. 354: Maladies de l'appareil digestif, chirurgie abdominale	73-642399	#1071291

525 SUPPLEMENT NOTE

I. UNNAMED SUPPLEMENTS

1.	Zoologische Jahrbücher. Abteilung für Systematik, Ökologie und Geographie der Tiere	82-645525	#1770666
2.	Hudson communiqué	sc83-2320	#8448188
3.	The Proletarian line	79-915582	#8655665
4.	Neurobehavioral toxicology and teratology	81-642303	#7088111
5.	Bio-bibliografía boliviana	79-648775	#3020266
6.	The Arup journal	sc83-7004	#8838510
7.	GeoJournal	78-642013	#3693750
8.	Bulletin of the World Health Organization. Supplement.	sf84-8025	#1840748
9.	Chandigarh Administration gazette	78-645952	#8363808
10.	World aviation directory	sc76-349	#2413063
11.	Czechoslovakia. Ministerstvo zdravotnictví. Věstník Ministerstva zdravotnictví	67-59180	#5080127
12.	New Zealand. Dairy Board. Annual report and statement of accounts	73-644668	#1787528
13.	Mining Symposium. Annual Mining Symposium	48-36897	#9616899
14.			
15.	New England economic almanac	sc82-7553	#7104447
16.	General embryological information service	sn83-10929	#1779150
17.	Organization for Economic Cooperation and Development. OECD financial statistics	78-642704	#1841149
18.	The Nursing journals index	83-644137	#9635534
19.	Quarterly economic review of China, North Korea	82-647227	#8277176
20.	Online terminal/microcomputer guide & directory	82-646619	#8066384
21.	American men of science	6-7326	#1354617
22.	Statisztikai évkönyv	58-16707	#1224981
23.	The American philatelist	8-22708	#1480549
24.	Angewandte Chemie (Weinheim an der Bergstrasse, Germany)	13-3396	#5845277

25.	Encyclopedia of associations	76-46129	#1223579
26.	Environmental science & technology	68-5797	#1568096
27.	ABMEES	82-646096	#7140542
28.	IDF standards and documents issued as supplements		#1753497
29.	Industrial diamond review	56-2274	#1645049
30.	Dalīl al-kitāb al-Miṣrī	72-960043	#3799080
31.	Archives de philosophie	84-641660	#1772219

II. NAMED SUPPLEMENTS (NOT PUBLISHED SEPARATELY)

1.	Corail (Noumea, New Caledonia : 1980)	sn82-21410	#7493588
2.			
3.	French studies	52-52554	#1242098
4.	3-trend security charts	73-640821	#6180538
5.	United States. President. Economic report of the President transmitted to the Congress	47-32975	#1193149
6.	Encyclopedia of American associations	59-6963	#1223565
7.	Center for Creative Photography (Series)	sn82-21382	#3338330

III. SPECIAL ISSUES

1.	Southern poetry review	sf83-5039	#9790536
2.	Women Library Workers (U.S.). Women library workers	sc83-7002	#2864777
3.	JEI report	sn82-20877	#7077306
4.	Musical America	cau07-4415	#1642199
5.	Abstract bibliography on coconut		#9424063
6.	International journal of physical distribution and materials management	82-646080	#3760812
7.	Evaluation and change	sc82-8179	#6504146
8.	Journal de physique. Lettres	sn82-8462	#1644319
9.	Landscape & turf industry	82-646507	#6441588
10.	Graphic arts monthly and the printing industry	sc82-5298	#3780884
11.	Pipeline & gas journal	sc83-7170	#7267775

IV. UPDATES

1.	Accounting standards, current text as of . . .	sc83-1081	#8833908
2.	Approved prescription drug products with therapeutic equivalence evaluations	sc82-7129	#7074861
3.	Book publishers directory	82-640252	#3231742
4.	Guide to U.S. Government publications	74-646648	#1795366
5.	Directory of corporate affiliations	83-641510	#1221072
6.	Directory of corporate affiliations of major corporations	83-641774	#1221060
7.	Physicians' desk reference	82-642489	#1311259
8.	United States. Federal Aviation Administration. Federal aviation regulations. Part 39, Airworthiness directives	81-640689	#4021147
9.	Exporters' encyclopaedia. World marketing guide	82-641772	#6138540
10.	Habitat preservation abstracts		#6676478
11.	Bibliography of society, ethics and the life sciences	73-160650	#1784518
12.	EIA publications directory, a user's guide	80-645059	#6307287
13.	Handbook of accounting and auditing	sn83-10351	#7756639
14.	Gazetteer of Canada	ce76-32235	#2627395
15.	International marketing handbook	sn82-6673	#8119702
16.	Commission of the European Communities. Library Luxembourg. EF-publikationer og dokumenter modtaget af Biblioteket	sn84-10430	#8963341
17.	United States. National Highway Traffic Administration. Driver licensing laws annotated	sn83-11723	#9142401
18.	Datapro directory of microcomputer software	sn82-788	#7636998

V. ACCOMPANYING INFORMATION

1.
2. Alinorm   81-649265   #1650325
3. International Joint   83-643527   #9025749
   Commission. Biennial
   report under the Great
   Lakes Water Quality
   Agreement of 1978
4. Health manpower provincial   76-642439   #2580880
   report, Manitoba
5. United States. Dept. of the   83-642416   #5869414
   Interior. National Park
   System new area studies,
   threatened landmarks and
   nationally significant
   historic places
6. The 5-year outlook on science   82-647246   #8767643
   and technology
7. Equal employment opportunity   82-646840   #8506032
   in the federal courts
8. New Jersey administrative   83-642713   #8960395
   reports
9. Tōyō Sōda kenkyū hōkoku   83-641671   #9277544
10. Encyclopedia of American   59-6963   #1223565
    associations
11. National Institutes of Health   sn83-11998   #8948406
    (U.S.). The medical staff
    fellowship program at the
    National Institutes of
    Health
12. Flood control project   79-644725   #5762082
    maintenance and
    repair . . . inspection
    report
13. Flood control project   79-644725   #5762082
    maintenance and
    repair . . . inspection
    report
14. Canadian oil & gas handbook   81-642832   #7078135
15. Antropologiska studies   83-642541   #7914928
16. Flue   sc82-4472   #8150495
17. Software publishers'   sn83-4375   #9952310
    catalogs annual
18. Alcheringa   sn83-10106   #7821635

530 ADDITIONAL PHYSICAL FORMS AVAILABLE NOTE

1.	IEE proceedings. G, Electronic circuits and systems	82-643911	#6046660
2.	Nuclear technology/fusion	81-641143	#6831387
3.	AEDC journal	82-644135	#7134111
4.	Advances in space research	83-645550	#7004415
5.	The Journal for special educators	80-644999	#4409595
6.	Journal of experimental psychology. Human learning and memory	76-643081	#1172614
7.	Library of Congress. Subject Cataloging Division. Subject headings in microform	79-641066	#3454199
8.	Computational linguistics (Association for Computational Linguistics (U.S.))		#11322424
9.	Employment fact book, for the period . . .	80-648102	#6522950

533   PHOTOREPRODUCTION NOTE

1.
2. The Reporter for   sc83-9165   #4531001
        conscience' sake
3. Statisticheski godishnik na   sc82-8195   #8776525
        Narodna Republika
        Bŭlgariĭa
4. Vocational education   sc82-7260   #4650443

546 LANGUAGE NOTE

I. LANGUAGE OF TEXT

1. Pharmatherapeutica — sn82-4598 — #2145498
2. Library of Congress. Library of Congress Office, New Delhi. Accessions list, South Asia — sc83-3005 — #8961462
3.
4. Acta cartographica — 68-7512 — #1460858
5. The China book & address directory — sc82-7310 — #4011437
6. Water-in-plants bibliography — sc83-5214
7. Orient — 83-644299 — #2679292
8. Anuário estatístico (Macao. Repartição dos Serviços de Estatística) — 83-642844 — #5041852
9. Bulletin trimestriel de la Société belge de photogrammétrie et de télédétection — 82-643582 — #8351882
10. Canadian review of physical anthropology — cn80-30468 — #6244471
11. The Tax/benefit position of selected income groups in OECD member countries — sc82-7588 — #7208615
12. Landbrugsmarkeder. Priser (Annual) — sc84-1005 — #8299572
13.
14. Acadiensis — cn77-318838 — #1670823
15. Acta pathologica et microbiologica Scandinavica. Section C: Immunology — sc76-423 — #1399249
16. Studi germanici — 82-646613 — #1766653
17. Manitoba modern language journal — cn83-30181 — #9414391
18. Boerhaave cahiers — sc82-5046 — #8416588
19. Argile — sc83-6089 — #1268486
20.

21.	Canada. Parliament. House of Commons. Subcommittee of the Standing Committee on External Affairs and National Defense on Canada's Relations with Latin America and the Caribbean. Subcommittee of the Standing Committee on External Affairs and National Defense on Canada's Relations with Latin America and the Caribbean : [minutes of proceedings and evidence]	82-640557	#8097307
22.	Canada. Dept. of Fisheries and Oceans. Report of operations under the Fisheries Development Act for the fiscal year ended Mar. 31 . . .	81-645480	#7805054
23.	Canada. Transport Canada. Annual report	83-643545	#8714973
24.	Bundesanstalt für Geowissenschaften und Rohstoffe. Tätigkeitsbericht	76-648862	#2767029
25.	Government of Canada internal energy conservation program	80-640412	#5018287
26.	International Centre for the Study of the Preservation and the Restoration of Cultural Property. Newsletter	sc83-2255	#6624877
27.			
28.	Kukche munwha	84-640956	#2263039

II. SUMMARY INFORMATION

1.	Anuário (Instituto Boliviano de Biología de Altura)	82-643788	#8539728
2.	Abbay	80-646507	#6825901
3.	Abhandlungen des Naturwissenschaftlichen Vereins in Hamburg	sn82-309	#7547018
4.	Acta Universitatis Lodziensis. Folia oeconomica	sn82-21898	#8125367

5.	Chūgoku gogaku	84-640440	#3134171
6.	Kontakt (Paris, France)	83-644172	#9492349
7.	Avian pathology	sn83-342	#2199397
8.	Gedrag	83-642254	#1185079
9.	Gelişme dergisi		#5583278
10.	Annales de microbiologie. B		#2257525
11.	Acta medica iranica		#1460918
12.	Les Carnets de l'enfance	68-348	#1241999
13.	Garcia de Orta	58-20407	#1570413
14.	Neophilologica	82-641207	#7937380
15.	Akita igaku	sc83-2756	#8742651
16.	International journal of sport psychology	82-646974	#1753592
17.	Zoologische Jahrbücher. Abteilung für Anatomie und Ontogenie der Tiere	82-645526	#1645063
18.	Jugoslavenska akademija znanosti i umjetnosti. Institut u Zadru. Radovi	58-20476	#1782815
19.	Postverket (Sweden)	78-642683	#3108753

III. TRANSLATION INFORMATION

1.	Revista nacional de telecomicações (International edition)	82-643575	#8072118
2.	Tradition médicale chinoise	sc82-5262	#8653846
3.	Artful dodge	sn80-134	#5872806

550   ISSUING BODIES NOTE

I.   GENERAL ISSUING BODY NOTES

1.	Checklist of official Pennsylvania publications	82-641505	#2259176
2.	Detailed mortality statistics, Alabama	82-643453	#5719288
3.			
4.	Current industrial reports. ITA-9008, Copper controlled materials	80-644856	#4506691
5.	Encuesta nacional de bovinos, X région, prov. Osorno	82-643772	#8537543
6.	Control of Power Systems Conference & Exposition. Conference record	82-642090	#3597953
7.			
8.	EACRATANAL information	sc83-6382	#8333682
9.	Current issue outline	82-645448	#6492410
10.	British Crop Protection Conference - Weeds. Proceedings of the British Crop Protection Conference	sn80-13359	#3949267
11.	Audiovisual materials	80-648903	#4782873
12.	Annual report to the legislature on the mandatory vehicle inspection program (MVIP)	sc83-1150	#9013972
13.	Gulf Coast Association of Geological Societies. Transactions	52-24459	#7887134
14.	Geological Survey (U.S.). Hydrologic investigations atlas	sn82-185	#1166303
15.	Pacific review (San Diego, Calif.)	83-647093	#9834503
16.	Australian journal of developmental disabilities	sn81-4344	#6720282
17.	Geological Survey (U.S.). Water Resources Division. Ground-water levels in observation wells in Arkansas	82-647378	#9086425

18.	Labour arbitration cases, 3rd ser.	sn82-22122	#8103793
19.	Annual report of the business done in pursuance of the Pension (Teachers) Act	81-649232	#8001151
20.	Agricultural finance outlook	80-644040	#5791912
21.	Nihon no bōei. English. Defense of Japan	83-646218	#5926190
22.	Current concepts in allergy and clinical immunology	sc83-2185	#3527242
23.	Fandom directory	sn82-22238	#7344904

II. PUBLISHER INFORMATION

1.	Acta chemica Scandinavica	49-28499	#981859
2.	Evaluation and change	sc82-8179	#6504146
3.	Asian outlook	65-9952	#1514436
4.	Onomastica Slavogermanica	a66-279	#5912743
5.	Inter-American music bulletin	pa57-186	#1588355
6.	Chung-kuo ching chi nien chien	83-642076	#8393846
7.	Alcheringa (New York, N.Y.)	72-626511	#1780749
8.	Annual review of jazz studies	82-644466	#8099505
9.	German chemical engineering	sn82-20491	#4441440
10.	Information series (Colorado Geological Survey)	sf82-3133	#2129065
11.	International journal of hospitality management	82-643994	#7827955
12.	The Stalnaker chronicles	84-642804	#10729656
13.	Advances in test anxiety research	83-640266	#9135225
14.	Oxford journal of legal studies	83-645842	#7636038

III. OFFICIAL ORGAN, PUBLICATION, ETC.

1.	Arts & architecture	46-32251	#1514368
2.	The Dance journal	82-643577	#4877180
3.	Forest industries (Auckland, N.Z.)	sc82-4222	#8101814
4.	Africa calls from Rhodesia	sf82-3147	#8754333
5.	Improving human performance quarterly	sc78-82	#2921859
6.	Annales de géographie	sn79-9782	#3341949
7.	Fruit world & market grower	sn84-10241	#7506093
8.	In situ (Lusaka, Zambia)	82-646728	#8971731

IV. VARIANT NAMES

1. Ya'ltyo p̣yā beḥérāwi bānk. 81-649424 #6527161
   Annual report
2.
3. Monograph (Foundation for 78-14367 #2245810
   Australian Literary
   Studies)
4. The Inter-allied review sf83-3024
5. Environmental satellite sc78-856
   imagery
6. U.S. directory of environmental sn79-5033 #5052744
   sources
7. Health manpower provincial 76-642439 #2580880
   report, Manitoba
8. Technical report (Skipjack sn83-10411 #8541060
   Survey and Assessment
   Programme)

555   CUMULATIVE INDEX NOTE/FINDING AIDS

I.   TABULAR NOTES

1.	Pacific sociological review	sn83-11258	#7131294
2.	Columbia Society of Inter-national Law. Bulletin	sc83-1000	#3529661
3.	The Journal of law and economic development	sn83-3988	#9244370
4.	American Oriental Society. Journal of the American Oriental Society	12-32032	#1480509
5.	Blake	78-642274	#3160132
6.	Change	80-643795	#1553876
7.	Biological reviews of the Cambridge Philosophical Society	sf84-8007	#3674460
8.	The Harvard International Law Club bulletin	sc84-1048	#7898463
9.	Zapiski Rossiĭskogo mineralogicheskogo obshchestva	sf83-5009	#8426157
10.	PN review (Manchester, England : 1979)	sc83-4179	#6000393
11.	Transactions of the Indiana State Medical Association	45-51152	#1588959
12.	Hanging loose	83-640340	#1877219
13.	Science of religion bulletin	sn82-21840	#7473942

II.   INFORMAL NOTES

1.	Annales de géographie	sn79-9782	#3341949
2.	Food & nutrition		#7081733
3.	Allgemeine deutsche Bibliothek	7-23735	#1479144
4.	Biochemistry abstracts. Part 1: Biological membranes	sc82-7512	#6001716
5.	Bulletin of prosthetics research	sn84-11428	#1537770
6.	Journal of marketing research	sc82-4518	#3808338
7.	Progress in inorganic chemistry	59-13035	#1645674
8.	Advances in polymer science	82-644437	#2256985

9.	Great Britain. Parliament. House of Commons. Parliamentary debates (Hansard). Offical report	10-3568	#8985610
10.	Moccasin telegraph (Canadian School Library Association)	cn81-311099	#2068331
11.	The Menges Family Association in America	83-643951	#9599842
12.	New special libraries	sn79-7093	#4069542
13.	American Society for Testing and Materials. Annual book of ASTM standards	83-641658	#2187052
14.	Resources in education	75-644211	#2241688
15.	Inland bird banding	82-647359	#5055631
16.	Nordicom	79-646477	#4030466
17.	Federal evaluations : a directory	82-640705	#7018279

580   LINKING ENTRY COMPLEXITY NOTE

I.   GENERAL LINKING NOTES

A.   Absorptions
1.	Scott chronicle of new issues	sn83-7211	#8981078
2.			
3.	Öl und Kohle	sn83-5728	#9659417
4.	Arts & architecture	46-32251	#1514368
5.	American metal market	12-805	#2239054
6.	Industrial diamond review	56-2274	#1645049
7.	British union-catalogue of periodicals	66-1557	#2049137

B.   Continuations
1.	AA guide to motoring in Kenya	81-645674	#4369708
2.	Journal of geophysical research. Oceans and atmospheres	83-641460	#3918273
3.			
4.	Journal of materials science		#1754660
5.	Bulletin of the American Museum of Natural History	12-30245	#1287364
6.	National Association of Retail Druggists. NARD journal	80-644613	#1695474
7.	American Society of Heating, Refrigerating and Air-Conditioning Engineers. ASHRAE handbook & product directory	73-644272	#1787246
8.	Acta embryologiae et morphologiae experimentalis (Halocynthis Association)	sc82-7167	#7302987
9.	Bibliographic guide to law	79-642569	#2282334
10.	Arid lands abstracts	sn80-402	#5983617
11.	Annual energy outlook		#9587622
12.	American men and women of science. The physical and biological sciences		#5464206
13.	Corail (Noumea, New Caledonia : 1980)	sn82-21410	#7493588
14.	Directory of State, county and Federal officials	74-644932	#1794151

15.	1001 home/decorating ideas	82-641478	#7181850
16.	Advance data from vital & health statistics of the National Center for Health Statistics	79-643688	#2778178
17.	Balance of payments statistics	sc82-7397	#7154626
18.	American Society of Civil Engineers. Water Resources Planning and Management Division. Journal of the Water Resources Planning and Management Division	76-645470	#2200366
19.	Statistics of Western Australia : non-rural primary industries	75-644517	#2241891
20.	Chicago Transit Authority. Annual report	82-644073	#8576106
21.	Les Carnets de l'enfance	68-348	#1241999

C. Mergers

1.	New scientist and science journal	82-644453	#2378327
2.	IEE proceedings. G, Electronic circuits and systems	82-643911	#6046660
3.	The Etude and musical world	sf83-8013	#9077596
4.	Social science & medicine. Part F, Medical & social ethics	81-646068	#6681754
5.	Acta botanica Barcinonensia	sn82-20968	#4533507

D. Miscellaneous general linking notes

1.	Annales de paléontologie (Paris, France : 1982)		#8770809
2.	Personal property security act cases	83-645286	#9046972
3.	Garcia de Orta	58-20407	#1570413

II. CUMULATIONS, SUMMARIES, ETC.

1.	Serials in the British Library	sc83-6318	#7979766
2.	NIH consensus development conference summary	sn80-589	#6038498
3.	British technology index (Annual)	63-23735	#1028311

4.	Serials in the British Library (Annual)	sn84-10171	#8264921
5.	Advances in behaviour research and therapy (Annual cumulation)	sc83-7092	#9165059
6.	Physical education index (Annual)	82-644892	#7890091
7.	Bell & Howell Co. Indexing Center. Bell & Howell's newspaper index to the Washington post	80-640592	#5972290
8.	Joint acquisitions list of Africana (Annual cumulation)	84-647202	#6654709
9.			
10.	Biogenic amines and trans- mitters in the nervous system	sc79-4875	#4939815
11.	Current technology index : CTI	81-644003	#7378113
12.	Telegen reporter	84-643679	#8377799
13.	Economics selections	83-643807	#2438009
14.	The Gramophone popular record catalogue		#4571281
15.	Bell & Howell's newspaper index to the Washington post	sn79-9720	#5528809
16.	Water resources data for Colorado	68-60770	#1159412
17.	Audiovisual materials	80-648903	#4782873
18.	International marketing handbook	sn82-6673	#8119702
19.	Los Angeles County wage and salary and civilian labor force employment estimate	sc83-7706	#9870778
20.	The Annual insider index to public policy studies	83-644562	#9212455
21.	Direction of trade statistics. Yearbook	82-646788	#7866916
22.	Current awareness profile on phase-transfer reactions	sn81-4022	#7427838
23.	Current awareness profile on electrostatic and hydro- phobic interactions in macromolecules	sn81-3793	#7251876

24.	Gas data book		#1203693
25.	The Quarterly index Islamicus	79-645142	#3415908
26.	National monthly medicaid statistics	81-642502	#6924357

III. EDITIONS

A. Language

1.	Assistance League of Southern California. News	82-644230	#8578901
2.	Présence africaine	51-31032	#1639236
3.	Meridiane 12-23	sc82-5224	#8692536
4.	Telcom report	81-644095	#4326720
5.	Āfāq (Giv'at Ḥavivah, Israel)	83-642884	#9449680
6.	Canadian Nuclear Society. Conference. Transactions	81-645711	#7802485
7.			
8.	Arab Bank for Economic Development in Africa. al-Taqrir al-sanawī	83-640302	#9142349

B. Miscellaneous edition information

1.	SIGCAPH newsletter	sc83-8561	#2054033
2.	Bell & Howell Co. Indexing Center. Bell & Howell's newspaper index to the Chicago Tribune	80-647862	#6796973
3.	Farm journal (Philadelphia, Pa. : 1956)	82-645584	#5843575
4.	U.S. information Moscow	sc82-4485	#8067779
5.	Journey (Dee Why West, A.C.T.)	sc83-2224	#9344181
6.	Information industry market place	81-643678	#7004484
7.	Beiträge zur Geschichte der deutschen Sprache und Literatur	01-16684	#1587656
8.	The Hammond almanac of a million facts, records, forecasts	79-642716	#4684127

IV. PREVIOUSLY PUBLISHED ELSEWHERE

A. Reprints
1.	The Armchair detective	82-643921	#8556372
2.	Jahrbuch der deutschen Sozialdemokratie für das Jahr . . .	sc82-4231	#8300186
3.	Art in America. Annual guide to galleries, museums, artists	83-640849	#9179141
4.	China. Chien she wei yüan hui. Chien she wei yüan hui kung pao	82-642240	#8996074
5.	Academy of Accounting Historians. Working paper series	sn83-10057	#4874242
6.	Colónida	82-647145	#9055962
7.	Nosotros (Mexico City, Mexico : 1912)	83-643751	#7918686
8.	La Falange	81-646413	#6912976
9.	Arxiu de tradicions populars recollides a Catalunya, Valencia, Mallorca, Rosselló, Sardenya, Andorra i terres aragoneses de parla catalana	80-649045	#6839654
10.	Locus	78-648218	#4386151
11.	The Floating bear	74-648009	#3704931
12.	Dav	82-644154	#6204769
13.	Owari no iseki to ibutsu	83-643221	#9503794
14.	Ulises (Mexico City, Mexico)	82-643062	#7918688
15.	Trends and perspectives in parasitology	81-642963	#7654173
16.	The Annual of American architecture	81-640394	#7082973
17.	Geochemistry (Chinese Society of Mineralogy, Petrology, and Geochemistry)	83-642398	#8618622
18.	American Heart Association monograph	sf81-1017	#1695120
19.	Gulf Coast Association of Geological Societies. Transactions	52-24459	#7887134

20.	Mémoires de la Société ffrigourgeoise des sciences naturelles. Géologie et géographie	sf83-9037	#1716293
21.	Kansas working papers in linguistics	sc84-1528	#5106933
22.	New York Law School journal of international and comparative law	83-640098	#6827154
23.	Cousins et cousines	83-645723	#4299364
24.	Memphis State University law review	75-649856	#1757101
25.	Computing reviews	66-98189	#1564620
26.	Writings on American history	4-8590	#1770230

B. Miscellaneous previous publication notes

1.	Micro/apple	83-645163	#7123088
2.	Copyright law decisions	sn83-10184	#8155172
3.	Quarterly coal report (United States. Energy Information Administration. Office of Coal, Nuclear, Electric, and Alternate Fuels)	sc83-1108	#8911051
4.	United States directory of federal regional structure	81-644317	#6922593
5.	Writings on American history	4-8590	#1770230
6.	Library of Congress. Congressional Research Service. Annual report of the Congressional Research Service of the Library of Congress for fiscal year . . . to the Joint Committee on the Library, United States Congress	72-624921	#2535916
7.	City government finances in . . .	74-648912	#1796776
8.	Tropical Pastures Program. Tropical Pastures Program annual report	sn83-10336	#7219044
9.	Industrial wastes (Chicago, Ill. : 1971)	82-646131	#2038241

10.	Annual report, occupational and professional licensing boards	82-645073	#7508074
11.	Index to plant chromosome numbers (St. Louis, Mo.)	sc82-7104	#8119053
12.	Lettere al Nuovo cimento	75-14184	#1755798
13.	Interiorscape	sn82-5163	#8338503
14.	Directory of auto supply chains	82-643079	#7979782
15.	The JWB circle	48-10402	#1923735
16.	Guide for hospital buyers	sn82-1001	#7083516
17.	The Gray's-Inn journal		#8404360
18.	Financial assistance by geographic area (United States. Dept. of Education. Office of Financial Management)	81-642167	#7539793
19.	Biologia medica (Istituto nazionale di chemioterapia (Italy))	sc82-2494	#8653221
20.	Royal Society (Great Britain). Council. Report of Council for the year ended 31 August . . .	81-642441	#7032235
21.	Federal Reserve Bank of Philadelphia. Annual report	18-26424	#1295599
22.	Felt and damaging earthquakes	83-644775	#6440198
23.	OECD financial statistics. Methodological supplement	83-647572	#8523788
24.	Annual energy summary	83-640229	#8598524
25.	Allg. Österr. Frauenverein. Jahresbericht des Allg. Österr. Frauenvereines	sc82-3686	#7503161
26.	Annual energy outlook		#9587622
27.	International labour review	sn83-4074	#5345843
28.	National Association of Retail Druggists. NARD newsletter	78-645112	#4102933

V. SPECIFIC AND NONSPECIFIC RELATIONSHIPS

A. Specific number(s) or issue(s)
1. Euromoney five hundred   82-646470   #8585694
2. American Association of   82-646586   #8446286
    Housing Educators. Con-
    ference. Proceedings
    of the . . . annual con-
    ference
3. Training marketplace directory   sn84-10287   #8843266
4. American Mathematical   13-24071   #5586858
    Society. List of officers
    and members
5. Outlook (Philadelphia, Pa.)   82-647121   #8508874
6. Garden design   82-647188   #8610163
7. Inventory of population   76-641286   #2475358
    projects in developing
    countries around the world
8. Public Relations Society of   sn83-10568   #7781945
    America. PRSA directory
9. Nursing job news nursing job   sn79-4698   #4252505
    guide to over 7,000
    hospitals
10. Bibliography of Asian studies   73-617426   #4285212
11. Soybean digest bluebook   sc82-1455   #5962597
12. American Library Association.   73-617320   #1415962
     ALA handbook of
     organization
13. Histoire littéraire du Québec   83-642183   #7669552
14. Federal Reserve Bank of   18-26424   #1295599
     Philadelphia. Annual
     report
15. American economic review   sc82-7551   #3637641
16. Funde und Ausgrabungen   sc83-5046   #8966929
     im Bezirk Trier
17. Drake law review   sc83-8510   #1566926
18. Federal Deposit Insurance   sc83-7079   #9094778
     Corporation. Annual
     report.

B. Nonspecific number(s) or issue(s)
1. Association of Engineering   #2256644
    Geologists. Directory
2.
3. Telephone directory of instru-   sn83-10326   #7345182
    mentation, equipment, and
    supplies

4.	Theochem	82-641126	#7073454
5.	Association for Childhood Education International. ACEI exchange	82-642762	#8229035
6.	Canadian weekend	cn80-30635	#6264679
7.	Scott chronicle of new issues	sn83-7211	#8981078
8.	Die Makromolekulare Chemie. Rapid communications	81-642667	#6241230
9.	Religion in America	sn83-10128	#6745609
10.	Advertising age. 100 leading markets	sc84-1229	#10249335
11.	Apparel industry magazine. Sourcebook	83-641522	#7360894

C. Companion volumes

1.	Acronyms, initialisms & abbreviations dictionary	81-643188	#2516185
2.	Reverse acronyms, initialisms, & abbreviations dictionary	sn80-13153	#4416864
3.	Collier bankruptcy cases	75-643843	#2241453
4.	Typological studies in language	sn84-10367	#10388792

D. Indexes

1.	Index of mathematical papers	72-624335	#1752735
2.	Government reports annual index	76-648535	#1781413
3.	Name of applicants for the registration of trade marks	82-641867	#8289687
4.	Curriculum development library. Cumulative index	sn83-10187	#6677031

E. Issued with

1.	DA, West Asia report	sn82-22066	#6247427
2.	Legal times of Washington (1982)	82-643347	#8239960
3.	Barron's index	76-640128	#1984310
4.	International aerospace abstracts	65-56077	#1696171
5.	Methodological surveys B : Biochemistry	83-3072	#5826981
6.	Studies in American Jewish literature	77-649500	#2747242

F. Supplements

1.	Directory of corporate affiliations	83-641510	#1221072
2.	Cerrahpaşa medical review	sc83-4105	#8983811
3.	Nature. Directory of biologicals	82-647157	#8042438
4.	Industrie minérale. Les techniques	sn82-20428	#6400380
5.	Business screen (New York, N.Y.)	82-644834	#7356032
6.	Books from Pakistan : [annual supplement]	72-930995	#1774265
7.	Directory information service	77-641771	#3208182
8.	Books in print microfiche publishers and distributors directory	sc82-7538	#8456803
9.	Instrument manufacturing. The . . . buyers' guide	46-5138	#8816047
10.	International Brain Research Organization. IBRO news	83-646493	#2001973
11.	Association of Engineering Geologists. Directory		#2256644
12.	Die Technik	49-4151	#2058956
13.	Journal of the Association for Computing Machinery	sc83-8125	#5098193
14.	State legislative leadership, committees, and staff	79-644269	#5123302
15.	Encyclopedia of associations	76-46129	#1223579
16.	Custom house guide	sc79-2690	#1199183

G. Updates

1.	America buys	81-642345	#6559169
2.	The Foundation directory	60-13807	#918159
3.	Acronyms, initialisms, & abbreviations dictionary		#2516185
4.	Directory of the American right	sn78-6891	#4455516
5.	Annual index to the Financial times	sc83-5049	#8726062
6.	Handbook for employees transferring to Spain	sn82-21039	#7185680
7.	Law . . . information	83-643008	#9151843
8.	Key indicators (Port-Vila, Vanuatu)	84-642364	#9175796
9.	Corporate giving watch	sc82-7555	#8123791

10.	Going public handbook	sn82-2005	#8168532
11.	Acronyms, initialisms & abbreviations dictionary	84-643188	#2516185

H. Miscellaneous specific and non-specific relationship notes

1.	Antitrust law & economics review	sf76-119	#1481629
2.	Economic analysis and workers' management	84-640698	#2337142
3.	Franchise opportunities		#7579012
4.	Travel trade directory	82-643714	#8525812

VI. "INCLUDES" STATEMENTS

1.	Datapro directory of small computers	sn81-4234	#7332427
2.	Outlook (Palo Alto, Calif.)	81-642508	#6878240
3.	Economic research report (Wine Institute (San Francisco, Calif.))	68-130950	#6903510
4.	Information & records management	83-645992	#1160980
5.	Transactions. Section C, Mineral processing & extractive metallurgy	sc82-7357	#2401167
6.	A.M. journal	sc83-3041	#8863499
7.	Pediatric infectious disease	sc82-7573	#7667444
8.	State education leader	83-640936	#8594394
9.			
10.	OLPR bulletin	sc81-3133	#2251560
11.	The Floating bear	74-648009	#3704931
12.	High fidelity (1980)	83-640343	#7081128
13.	Journal of financial and quantitative analysis	sc82-2518	#1066606
14.	Anali Historijskog odjela Centra za znanstveni rad Jugoslavenske akademije u Dubrovniku	79-645643	#5168622
15.	Metals and materials	sn82-22249	#1757192
16.	Healthcare financial management	83-642646	#8504366
17.	Standard & Poor's creditweek	82-640380	#7910037
18.	HFD/retailing home furnishings	78-648320	#2941404
19.	Coal report in Illinois	sc80-1080	#2371496

20.	The drug, the nurse, the patient	66-15620	#3995456
21.	The Journal of Asian studies	sn83-7017	#1713826
22.	Nation's cities	67-122855	#1759466
23.	Designers West	81-641142	#4087182
24.	Harris Ohio marketers industrial directory : MID	82-644198	#8021765
25.	Nuclear instruments & methods in physics research	81-643559	#7608866
26.	U.S. long-term review	82-645152	#8735951
27.	American journal of physiology	a43-3158	#1480180
28.	Banking	38-7912	#1519148
29.	American perfumer and aromatics	sc78-785	#2630124
30.	Annales de géographie	sn79-9782	#3441949
31.	City magazine annual	cn83-39017	#7411169
32.	Plant disease	79-643690	#4844576
33.	Science world	sn81-424	#7142779
34.	Institution of Mechanical Engineers (Great Britain). Proceedings	8-18925	#1753277
35.	Scott stamp monthly	83-641730	#8932842
36.	FLC newsletter	sf77-89	#2133488
37.	Annual report on carcinogens	80-647787	#6543913

VII. MISCELLANEOUS LINKING NOTES

1.	Transactions. Section B, Applied earth science	sc82-7356	#2401166
2.	Current drug handbook	58-6390	#1565622
3.	The Journal of the Institution of Engineers, Australia	sn79-5682	#2754484
4.	National Online Meeting. Proceedings	83-641045	#7626119
5.	Americana (New York, N.Y. : 1925)	25-23066	#2923293
6.	Acronyms, initialisms & abbreviations dictionary	84-643188	#2516185
7.	U.S. lodging industry. Digest	83-640330	#8968220
8.	International yearbook of education	49-48323	#1753766
9.	Orpheus (Norfolk, Conn.)	48-21925	#4250720

10.	Atlantic Provinces Linguistic Association. Meeting. Papers from the . . . annual meeting of the Atlantic Provinces Linguistics Association	82-640192	#7857905
11.	Ohio official reports	sn82-5967	#8610029
12.	Social security bulletin. Annual statistical supplement	sc77-385	#1939422

Suggested Readings

Cannan, Judith Proctor. **Special Problems in Serials Cataloging.** Washington, DC: Library of Congress, 1979, pp. 33-39.

These pages in Cannan's book deal with special problems a serials cataloger may encounter in the notes area of a catalog record. This information, as well as the information provided in the rest of the publication, is very helpful and clearly written but the cataloger must remember how rules and principles have changed since 1979 and be sure the recommendations are still current before applying them.

Cataloging & Classification Quarterly. Vol. 1, no. 1- . New York: Haworth Press, 1980- . Quarterly.

While this tool does not treat serials directly it is a good resource for keeping up-to-date on what's current in the area of cataloging, e.g., authority control, subject analysis, description, and AACR2.

Cataloging Service Bulletin. No. 1- . Washington, DC: Library of Congress, 1978- . Quarterly.

Catalog departments should provide individual subscriptions to this journal for their serials catalogers. Meant primarily for the descriptive and subject catalogers at LC, it keeps the cataloger abreast of cataloging practices at LC by providing rule interpretations and current subject heading practices, as well as information regarding LC classification.

Serials Librarian. Vol. 1, no. 1- . New York: Haworth Press, 1976- . Quarterly.

This journal is designed to provide articles, reviews, and news regarding all aspects of serials management and is a *must* for the informed serials cataloger.

Serials Review. Vol. 1, no. 1- . Ann Arbor, MI: Pierian Press, 1975- . Quarterly.

This is an authoritative and comprehensive publication providing reviews, papers, and bibliographies useful to all involved in the area of serials librarianship. *Serials Review* is a good companion journal to *Serials Librarian* and should be consulted on a regular basis.

Wynar, Bohdan S. **Introduction to Cataloging and Classification.** 7th ed. by Arlene G. Taylor. Littleton, CO: Libraries Unlimited, 1986, pp. 210-214.

This updated edition of a standard introductory textbook includes a chapter on serials that has been updated to conform with current AACR2 practices in the area of serials cataloging. The pages devoted to notes are particularly useful, providing good examples and clear rule interpretations.